First World War
and Army of Occupation
War Diary
France, Belgium and Germany

29 DIVISION
88 Infantry Brigade
Prince of Wales's Leinster Regiment (Royal Canadians)
2nd Battalion
1 February 1918 - 23 June 1919

WO95/2308/1

The Naval & Military Press Ltd
www.nmarchive.com
Published in association with The National Archives

Published by

The Naval & Military Press Ltd

Unit 10 Ridgewood Industrial Park,

Uckfield, East Sussex,

TN22 5QE England

Tel: +44 (0) 1825 749494

www.naval-military-press.com

www.nmarchive.com

This diary has been reprinted in facsimile from the original. Any imperfections are inevitably reproduced and the quality may fall short of modern type and cartographic standards.

© Crown Copyright
Images reproduced by permission of The National Archives, London, England, 2015.

Contents

Document type	Place/Title	Date From	Date To
Miscellaneous	WO95/2308/2		
Heading	29th Division 88th Infy Bde, 2nd Bn Leinster Regt 1918 Feb To June 1919 From 24 Div 73 Bde.		
Heading	16th Division 47th Infy Bde, 2nd Bn Leinster Regt Feb-Apl 1918		
Miscellaneous	War Diary For Month of February, 1918 Unit 2nd Btn Leinster Regiment Vol 43		
War Diary	Montigny Fm	01/02/1918	01/02/1918
War Diary	Tincourt	02/02/1918	02/02/1918
War Diary	Saulcourt	03/02/1918	03/02/1918
War Diary	Ronssoy	04/02/1918	08/02/1918
War Diary	Ken Lane	09/02/1918	12/02/1918
War Diary	Ronssoy	13/02/1918	14/02/1918
War Diary	Lancaster House	16/02/1918	24/02/1918
War Diary	Ronssoy	25/02/1918	28/02/1918
Heading	47th Brigade. 16th Division. 2nd Battalion The Leinster Regiment March 1918		
Heading	War Diary of 2nd Battalion The Leinster Regiment. From 1st March 1918. To 31st March, 1918. Vol 43 Vol 40		
War Diary		01/03/1918	20/03/1918
War Diary	Villers Faucon	21/03/1918	31/03/1918
Heading	War Diary of 2nd Battalion, Leinster Regiment. From 1st April, 1918 To 30th April, 1918 (Volume No. 1) Vol 44		
War Diary	Field	01/04/1918	30/04/1918
War Diary	War Diary of 2nd Battalion, Leinster Regiment. From 1st May, 1918 To 31st May, 1918 (Volume No. 2) Vol 45		
War Diary	Field	01/05/1918	31/05/1918
Operation(al) Order(s)	Operation Orders. No. 6 By Lieut. Col. H.W. Weldon. Commanding 2nd. Battn. The Leinster Regt.	19/05/1918	19/05/1918
Heading	Adjutant		
Operation(al) Order(s)	Operation Order No. 8. By Lt-Colonel H.W. Weldon., Commanding 2nd. Bn. Leinster Regt.	26/05/1918	26/05/1918
Operation(al) Order(s)	Operation Order No. 9. By Lieut-Colonel H.W. Weldon., Commanding 2nd. Bn. Leinster Regt.	30/05/1918	30/05/1918
Heading	War Diary of 2nd Battalion, The Leinster Regiment. From 1st June, 1918 To 30th June, 1918 (Volume No. 3) Vol 47		
Miscellaneous	29th Division No. 317/14	24/08/1918	24/08/1918
War Diary	In The Field	01/06/1918	30/08/1918
Operation(al) Order(s)	Operation Order No. 7. By Lieut. Col. H.W. Weldon., Commanding 2nd. Battn. Leinster Regt.	11/06/1918	11/06/1918
Heading	War Diary of 2nd Battalion The Leinster Regiment. From 1st July, 1918 To 31st July, 1918 (Volume No. 4) Vol 47		
War Diary	In The Field. Lumbres	01/07/1918	31/07/1918

Heading	War Diary of 2nd Battalion, The Leinster Regiment. From 1st August, 1918 To 31st August, 1918 (Volume No. 5) Vol 49		
War Diary	In The Field.	01/08/1918	31/08/1918
Operation(al) Order(s)	Operation Order No. 25 By Lieut. Col H.W. ?	20/08/1918	20/08/1918
Operation(al) Order(s)	Operation Orders No. 26 By Lt Col H.W. ? Commdg 2nd Regt.	23/08/1918	23/08/1918
Operation(al) Order(s)	Operation Order No. 27. By Capt V.J. Farrell M.C. Comdg 2nd Leinster Regt.	26/08/1918	26/08/1918
Operation(al) Order(s)	Operation Orders No. 29	30/08/1918	30/08/1918
Heading	War Diary of 2nd Battalion, The Leinster Regiment. From 1st September To 30th September, 1918 (Volume No 6). Vol 50		
War Diary	In The Field.	01/09/1918	30/09/1918
Heading	War Diary of 2nd Battalion The Leinster Regiment. From 1st October To 31st October, 1918 (Volume No. 7) Vol 49		
War Diary	Sheet 28 Gheluwe	01/10/1918	02/10/1918
War Diary	Brandhoek Area	03/10/1918	04/10/1918
War Diary	Ypres	05/10/1918	06/10/1918
War Diary	Westhoek	07/10/1918	08/10/1918
War Diary	Ledeghem Sector	09/10/1918	11/10/1918
War Diary	Becelaere Area.	12/10/1918	13/10/1918
War Diary	Ledeghem Area	14/10/1918	14/10/1918
War Diary	Sheet 29	14/10/1918	31/10/1918
Operation(al) Order(s)	Operation Order No. 35. By Lt Col H.W. Weldon., Comdg 2nd. Leinster Regt	06/10/1918	06/10/1918
Operation(al) Order(s)	Operation Order No. 36. By Lt Col H.W. Weldon Comdg 2nd Leinster Regt.	08/10/1918	08/10/1918
Operation(al) Order(s)	Operation Order No. 37	10/10/1918	10/10/1918
Operation(al) Order(s)	Operation Order No. 38. By Lt Col H.W. Weldon Comdg 2nd Leinster Regt.	11/10/1918	11/10/1918
Operation(al) Order(s)	Operation Orders No. 39. by Lieut. Colonel. H.W. Weldon., Commanding 2nd. Battalion Leinster Regiment.	13/10/1918	13/10/1918
Operation(al) Order(s)	Operation Orders No 40 Lieut Colonel H.W. Weldon Commanding 2nd Leinster Regt.		
Operation(al) Order(s)	Administrative Order No. 1 By Lieut. Colonel H.W. Weldon., Commanding 2nd. Battalion Leinster Regt.	13/10/1918	13/10/1918
Heading	War Diary of 2nd Battalion The Leinster Regiment. From 1st November To 30th November 1918 (Volume No. 8) Vol 51		
War Diary	Field	01/11/1918	01/11/1918
War Diary	Croix	01/11/1918	11/11/1918
War Diary	Ref. Tournai 5	12/11/1918	18/11/1918
War Diary	Ref Tournai 5 Brussels 5	19/11/1918	22/11/1918
War Diary	Ref. Brussels.5	23/11/1918	29/11/1918
War Diary	Liege 7	29/11/1918	29/11/1918
War Diary	Marche 9	30/11/1918	30/11/1918
Operation(al) Order(s)	Operation Order No. 40	07/11/1918	07/11/1918
Operation(al) Order(s)	Operation Order No. 41	17/11/1918	17/11/1918
Operation(al) Order(s)	Operation Order 42. By Lt Col H.W. Weldon. D.S.O., Comdg 2nd. Bn. Leinster Regt.	20/11/1918	20/11/1918
Operation(al) Order(s)	Operation Order 43. By Lt Col H.W. Weldon. D.S.O., Commanding 2nd. Bn. Leinster Regt.	22/11/1918	22/11/1918

Operation(al) Order(s)	Operation Order 44. By Lt Col H.W. Weldon. D.S.O., Commanding 2nd. Bn. Leinster Regt.	26/11/1918	26/11/1918
Operation(al) Order(s)	Operation Order 45. By Lt Col H.W. Weldon. D.S.O., Commanding 2nd. Bn. Leinster Regt.	27/11/1918	27/11/1918
Operation(al) Order(s)	Operation Order 46. By Lt Col H.W. Weldon. D.S.O., Comdg 2nd. Battn. Leinster Regt.	28/11/1918	28/11/1918
Operation(al) Order(s)	Operation Order 47. By Lt Col H.W. Weldon. D.S.O., Comdg 2nd. Battn. Leinster Regt.	29/11/1918	29/11/1918
Operation(al) Order(s)	Operation Order 48. By Lieut Col H.W. Weldon. D.S.O., Comdg 2nd. Battn. Leinster Regt.	30/11/1918	30/11/1918
Heading	War Diary of 2nd Battalion The Leinster Regiment From 1st December To 31st December, 1918 (Volume No. 9) Vol 52		
War Diary	Ref Marched Map	01/12/1918	04/12/1918
War Diary	Ref. M.I. Germany	04/12/1918	06/12/1918
War Diary	Ref. IM. IL. Germany.	07/12/1918	31/12/1918
Heading	Southern (Late 29th) Divn 88th Infy Bde 2nd Bn Leinster Regt Jan-Jun 1919		
Heading	War Diary of 2nd Battalion The Leinster Regiment. From 1st January To 31st January, 1919 (Volume No. 10) Vol 53		
War Diary	Dhunn	01/01/1919	13/01/1919
War Diary	Wermelskirchen	14/01/1919	31/01/1919
Heading	War Diary of 2nd Battalion The Leinster Regiment. From 1st February 1919 To 28th February, 1919 (Volume No. 11) Vol 54		
War Diary	Wermelskirchen	01/02/1919	28/02/1919
Heading	2nd Leinster Regiment. March 1919 Missing.		
War Diary	Mulheim	01/04/1919	06/04/1919
War Diary	Charlroi-Wargnies-Le-Petit	07/04/1919	07/04/1919
War Diary	Wargnies-Le-Petit	07/04/1919	30/04/1919
Miscellaneous	War Diary	05/04/1919	05/04/1919
War Diary	Wargnies Le Petit	01/05/1919	18/06/1919
War Diary	Le-Quesnoy-Cambrai	19/06/1919	19/06/1919
War Diary	Cambrai-Boulogne	20/06/1919	20/06/1919
War Diary	Boulogne	21/06/1919	23/06/1919

W0a5/2308/2

29TH DIVISION
86TH INFY BDE

(10 DIV 47.I.6.)

2ND BN LEINSTER REGT

~~MAY — DEC 1914~~

1918 FEB ~~1919~~ JUNE 1919

From 24 DIV 1.2.1418
73 Bde

16TH DIVISION
47TH INFY BDE

2ND BN LEINSTER REGT
FEB - APL 1918

WAR DIARY.

FOR MONTH OF FEBRUARY, 1918.

VOLUME:-

UNIT:- 2nd Btn Leinster Regiment

WAR DIARY or INTELLIGENCE SUMMARY.

Army Form C. 2118.

2/Bn LEINSTER REGT.

February 1918

Place	Date	Hour	Summary of Events and Information	Remarks and references to Appendices
Montigny	1.2.18		The battalion was addressed by Maj Gen Daly Cmdg 24th Division prior to departure. The battalion then marched to Tincourt when it was billetted for the night. The roads from Montigny that moment were known by those of other units of the 24th Division who had assembled to meet the battalion "en route" and "good luck". A Special Routine Order was published by Gen Daly on the occasion of the departure of "The finest fighting battalion".	MS
Tincourt	2.2.18		The battalion is now in the 16th Division commanded by Maj Gen Sir W.B. Hickie K.C.M.G. 47th Brigade commanded by Brig Genl H.O Gwynn. The battalion was addressed by Maj Genl Sir W. Hickie at Tincourt and then marched to Saulcourt where it was billetted for the night.	MS
Saulcourt	3.2.18		Church parade. The DGO inspected the Box Respiratory all ranks. The battalion relieved the 6th Royal Irish Regt in Bde Support at Ronssoy, and took over the Cadre nres of the Royal Irish Gassan. The battalion is billetted in cellars which are fairly dry and comfortable.	MS
Ronssoy	4.2.18		In Support. Battalion working parties on L'Empire defences. Fairly quiet day. Lt Col H.N. Weldon returned from leave and resumed command of battalion 24in to	MS

WAR DIARY
or
INTELLIGENCE SUMMARY

Army Form C. 2118.

Feby 1918

Place	Date	Hour	Summary of Events and Information	Remarks and references to Appendices
POPERINGHE	4.2.18		Shelly hospital. Also Lieuts Holmes & Tomey. Heavy artillery fire from both sides at Ypres	
"	5.2.18		In support. Capt Deverie to Hospital Sick. Capt Webb wounded (at duty). Office Leaving Shellas at 3.30pm. 2nd OR killed 5 OR wounded. Quiet night.	
"	6.2.18		Draft of 30 reinforcements arrived at Details Camp.	
"	7.2.18		15 Gunners and 15 Trans. to hospital. Usual working parties. Quiet day.	
"	8.2.18		Quiet day. Working parties in morning.	
"			Right subsection of (4)th Coy. Ashmed 9/th trenches. Enemy's attitude quiet. Very good trenches.	
KEMMEL	9.2.18		Quiet day. Capt L.S. Nathan acting Intelligence Officer.	
"	10.2.18		" " " Propaganda thrown into our trench near Gillmont. Mr Ferd attached to aerial dart enclosing Lloyd George's speech and appealing to Irishmen to desert from the British army. Sent in reply, a hurricane of Rifle grenades, and S.A.A in reply.	
"	11.2.18		Heavy Shelling at evening Stand-to. 500 shells of various calibres. No casualties.	

WAR DIARY or INTELLIGENCE SUMMARY

Army Form C. 2118.

Place	Date	Hour	Summary of Events and Information	Remarks and references to Appendices
KEN LANE	12/2/18		Relieved by 1st Royal Munster Fusiliers and moved to RONSSOY in Brigade Support. Intermittent shelling.	
RONSSOY	13/2/18		Nothing to report. Enemy shelling LEMPIRE & Officers (P) Heavy shelling of roads by A.A. guns increasing numbers of gas shells employed. Partly clear. TOMBOIS FARM Rd & then road W. of 1½ hour. No Casualties or distress.	
RONSSOY	14/2/18		Reinforcement of 15 officers and 300 other ranks from 1st Batt. Sandst. Regt. joined. Officers — Capts CRAIG, WELD, DENCH, Lieuts ROBB, COADE, KEATING & KIRKPATRICK, FARRELL, 2Lieuts SMYTH, LEMON, HERBERT, BOYER, O'BRIEN, HICKEY, FORREST, 2Lt 6th O'Brien appointed Intelligence officer with 6 Bn. L.S. MATHIAS and O/Rs to his Coy. Battn. sent patrols. Relieved the 6 Connaught Rangers in left subsector. Coys disposed as follows — D Coy. Right Front Line, "C" Left Front Line, B Support, A Reserve. Battn HQ at LANCASTER HOUSE.	

WAR DIARY
or
INTELLIGENCE SUMMARY.

(Erase heading not required.)

Army Form C. 2118.

Place	Date	Hour	Summary of Events and Information	Remarks and references to Appendices
LANCASTER HOUSE 20	16/5/18		2nd Lt. W.H. SPENCER appointed assistant Adjutant	
	17/5/18		Enemy's present lay and going heavy. One man wounded in front line. Enemy TMs. fairly quiet both by day & by night. Visual working badly.	
	18th		One Coy of 1st RMF raided enemy line at WILLOW TRENCH, and got as far as the support line (night 18/19th) – taking 5 prisoners & inflicting severe slight casualties. Enemy in ft line heavy on the night of 19/20th. Sentry moved to 2 nd & 3rd S the afternoon are 4 our planes attacked 5 hostile aeroplanes and drove them in over lines in N.E. Co. Still heavy	
	20th		Light bombardment of our front system and C.T.s from 2.30 – 6.30 P.M. enemy rifles and one wounded. Rifles and Sight	
	21st		raining during the evening Enemy again opened all calibres on forward system shelling very terrific and up the wagh Dave. During the morning a party of about 12 of the enemy attempted to approach our post	

WAR DIARY or INTELLIGENCE SUMMARY

Army Form C. 2118.

Place	Date	Hour	Summary of Events and Information	Remarks and references to Appendices
LANCASTER HOUSE	Feby 1918			
	22nd		In COCHRANE AVENUE via the old C.T. Our men Offrs reported at 30 yards range and Hay (the enemy) dumps etc. (Enemy) patrol immediately left our lines & returned to own lines. Some shelling of BURSOY & EMPIRE during the day.	/H
	23rd		One Infantry wounded. Enemy artillery fairly quiet. Patrol from A Coy under 2 Lt Holmes went out but had to lie in crater for a few enemy patrols which he suspected to work the old CT leading to COCHRANE AVENUE regularly. (2 saps of enemy below our post in the old C.T. Result - Enemy hollow post at A.9. L 11 b 5 3 & few sandbags placed. Some heavy shells on back areas in afternoon. 1200 on three row trench at B.8.9/B.8.9. Enemy sweeping aeroplane flew over the day. Our snipers claim two hits at A.9. b 10.40. Patrol of 2 L/Cpls O'Sullivan & Ward Coy (Lt 2/7 R 3 r). No enemy. 2 Lt O'Sullivan & 2 A/M E. Quinn L/Cpls go to BOURSOY for dinner as Brigade support	/H
	24th		Reliefs by 1 R.M.L. 5	/H

Army Form C. 2118.

WAR DIARY
or
INTELLIGENCE SUMMARY.
(Erase heading not required.)

Place	Date	Hour	Summary of Events and Information	Remarks and references to Appendices
ROSSOY	July 1918 24th		Enemy artillery unusually quiet. Activity seen below normal. Very quiet day.	
"	25th		Heavy shelling of CITADEL during the day. At midnight 24/25th shells fell on our front system during enemy activity against our right. Work on LEMPIRE defences and ECHO POST. Stunts signalled nothing on visual station (ROSSOY).	
"	26th			
"	27th		Lempire received a few shells in morning. ROSSOY WOOD intermittently shelled during the day. Work continues on LEMPIRE defences and visual station.	
"	28th		ROSSOY WOOD again shelled by 10.5 cms + 15 cms. Village also received attention in the forenoon. We relieve 6th Conn. Rangers in Right subsection, the typates relief by 2nd Lincolns not taking place. Operation orders being canalled by Batt. H.Q.. Coy dispos as follows 'A' Coy Left Front Line, 'B' Right Front Line, 'C' Support, 'D' Reserve. Reinforcements of 38 other ranks joined Battalion	

Martin Lt Col.
Cmndg 2nd Bn. LEINSTER REGT.

47th Brigade.

16th Division.

2nd BATTALION

THE LEINSTER REGIMENT

MARCH 1918

CONFIDENTIAL

WAR DIARY

of

2nd Battalion The Leinster Regiment.

From 1st March 1918.   To 31st March, 1918.

WAR DIARY or INTELLIGENCE SUMMARY

(Erase heading not required.)

M A R C H / 1918

2nd. Battn. Leinster Regiment.

Instructions regarding War Diaries and Intelligence Summaries are contained in F.S. Regs., Part II and the Staff Manual respectively. Title Pages will be prepared in manuscript.

Place	Date	Hour	Summary of Events and Information	Remarks and references to Appendices
	1/3/18		Battalion in Front Line, Right Sub Section. Nothing unusual.	
	2/3/18		Battalion in Front Line, Right Sub Section. Quiet Day.	
	3/3/18		2/Lieut. P.R. Farrelly M.C. & Lieut. W.H.Ceade admitted to Hospital.	
	3/3/18		Battalion in Front Line, Right Sub Section. Quiet Day. I O. R. Wounded Gun Shot. Lieut. M.C.E. Sharpe rejoined from Leave.	
	4/3/18.		Battalion in Front Line. Nothing unusual. Major J.R.Frend. (D.S.O.) Capt. D.P.A.McGann (M.C.) Capt. J.W.Webster proceeded on leave to U.K. 2/Lieut. W. McNamara admitted to Hospital Sick.	
	5/3/18		Battalion relieved in Front Line and proceeded to Bde. Support in GRANGE CAMP near VILLIERS FAUCON. Lieut. Col. H.E.Welden took over the duties of Brigadier General.	
	6/3/18.		2/Lieut. W.M.Surtees rejoined from duty at Base.	
	7/3/18) to		Lieut. W.G.Toomey proceeded to England for transfer to Indian Army.	
	13/3/18)		Battalion in Bde. Support. Working Parties 9 Officers & 300 O.Rs. on BROWN LINE.	
	14/3/18		Battalion in Bde. Support. Working Parties as for the 6th.	
	15/3/18		Battalion moved by march route to TINCOURT.	
	16/3/18		Battalion at TINCOURT.	
	17/3/18.		Battalion moved by lorries to GRANGE CAMP. St. PATRICK'S DAY. Sports held by Battalion.	
	18/3/18.		Battalion Grange Camp. Working Parties 9 Officers & 300 Other Ranks on BROWN LINE.	
	19/3/18		----- same as 18th.inst. - 2/Lieut. J.M.Hunter joined Battalion.	
	20/3/18		----- same as 18th.inst.	
VILLERS FAUCON	21/3/18.	4.45. a.m.	Enemy bombardment commenced. Battalion suffered many casualties by 9 a.m. STOOD TO under cover of embankment at GRANGE CAMP.	
		2.40.p.m.	Battalion ordered to BROWN LINE. Headquarters at SPUR QUARRY	
		6 p.m.	BROWN LINE occupied by Four Companies Element of enemy driven out. Right Company in touch with 66th. Div. TEMPLEUX WOOD left with Munster's.	
		10.30 p.m.	B.M. H.Q. moved to BROWN LINE SUPPORT from QUARRY.	
	22/3/18	7.30 a.m.	66th. Div. apparently retired exposing Right Flank. Enemy worked through Gap and inflicted heavy casualties on Right Company's. "A" & "B" Coys. forced to withdraw to position 500 yards in rear. About 9 a.m. Battalion reinforced by 2 Companies 11th. Sussex & 2 Tanks.	
		11 a.m.	Battalion forced to withdraw to Railway Cutting in E.29. - Railway Cutting enfiladed by Machine Guns.	

WAR DIARY or INTELLIGENCE SUMMARY

(Erase heading not required.)

Army Form C. 2118.

Place	Date	Hour	Summary of Events and Information	Remarks and references to Appendices
	22/3/18	11.30 a.m.	Battalion forced to withdraw to ridge SOUTH WEST of VILLIERS - FAUCON and occupied shallow trenches - by this time Major FREEMAN Commanding and all the Officers of the Battalion in the Battle Area with the exception of Lieut. KIRKPATRICK and Lieut Morrison had become casualties by 12 noon this position was rendered untenable not only by the enemy but by our own guns whose barrage was coming down on the ridge & trenches½ The two Right Coys ("A" & "B") had suffered severe casualties mostly from infilade fire from right rear.	
		12.30 p.m.	Remains of Battalion intermixed with Hants Pioneer and Unit of 39th. Div. withdrew to GREEN LINE at TINCOURT.	
		5 p.m.	Details of Battalion numbering 110 under Lieut. Kirkpatrick & Morrison re-organised into I Battalion with details of 2 Connaught Rangers and placed under Command of Lt.Col. Fielding D.S.O	
		7 p.m.	Composite Battalion took up position in SUPPORT of GREEN LINE on the HAMEL - TEMPLEUX - LA FOSS Road. East of Bois-de-BUIRE. The following casualties took place during the day. KILLED. Lieut. Craig.,2/Lt. Butler,2/Lt.Brophy.,2/Lt. Eastwood.,2/Lt.Surtees.,2/Lt,Stowell. WOUNDED. Major. Freeman,2/Lt.Cullinan,Capt.Barry.,Capt.Wild,Capt.Mathias,Lt.Doyle,2/Lt,Parks, 2/Lt. Taylor,2/Lt.Lemon(M.C.)2/Lt.Keogh,Fitzgerald,Herbert,Delaney,Hunter,O'Brien. MISSING. 2/Lieut. Smythe.	
	23/3/18	4 a.m.	Lieut.Kirkpatrick and 2/Lt.Morrison were relieved by Capt.Webster.,Lieut.Barnwell,Lt.Keating.	
		8 a.m.	Battalion received orders to cover the withdrawal of units of 49th. Bde holding the Green Line latter passed through & aided by fog. Battalion withdrew without casualties to positions on ridge in I.25 central Sheet 62 d/40,000. BIACHES	
	About	12.30 p.m.	Battalion ordered to withdraw to position W of BIACHES fighting rear-guard action. About 60 men under Capt. Webster passing along railway line S of ST. DENIS to HALLE and thence across the wooden bridge at RANIZCOURT over the canal to position for reorganization about 800 yards N.W. of BIACHES where they were joined by Lt.Col.Weldon acting B.G.C. 47th.INF.Bde Signal officer(Lt. Emily R.E.) and Lieut. Barnwell.- Capt. Webster cleared the wounded and reported with 49 men to Divisional Headquarters at HERBECOURT. The remainder of the Leinsters accompanied the Connaughts and passed through PERONNE and re-organized under Brigadier General Ramsay & Leverson Gower. Together with 73 Leinsters who had become detached the day previous and had joined up with units 39th.Divison.	
	24/3/18.M.N.		The 16th. Divison. were relieved and Leinster Regt. re-joined Transport about mile and half E of CAPPY - Battalion moved at 3.30 p.m. to camp 1 mile W of BRAY.	
		5 p.m.	Lt.Col. Weldon re-joined Battalion from command of Bde.- Battalion reorganized into 2 Coys under Capt. Webster and Capt. McCann½ Strength about 175¾	

Army Form C. 2118.

WAR DIARY
or
INTELLIGENCE SUMMARY.
(Erase heading not required.)

Instructions regarding War Diaries and Intelligence Summaries are contained in F. S. Regs., Part II. and the Staff Manual respectively. Title pages will be prepared in manuscript.

Place	Date	Hour	Summary of Events and Information	Remarks and references to Appendices
	24/3/18	5.30 p.m.	Battalion moved to CHIPPILLY and took over crossings of the SOMME CHIPPILLY and CERISY throwing out outpost of the ridge SOUTH.	
	25/3/18	4 p.m.	Battalion moved to MORCOURT and took over the defences of the Canal from Mericourt Central to ½ mile N.W. of Morcourt.	
	26/3/18	9 a.m.	Battalion moved to a position of assembly 1 mile S.W. of PROYART - "C" Coy under Capt. McCann at PROYART where they dug trenches under R.E. E of Railway cutting PROYART & S of PROYART - CHUIGNOLLES Rd. About 25 stragglers rejoined Battalion.	
	about	3 p.m.	Battalion took over trenches E of Railway Cutting PROYART. On the right Company of HERTS and 39th. Division on the left Connaught Rangers and Munsters. - Battalion dug themselves in and remained there for the night. Patrols were sent out and one Prussian was captured.	
	27/3/18	about 11 a.m.	Report received by O.C. Connaughts flank was being turned and Inflade M.G. Fire had been brought to bear on the embankment lived by that Unit the position became untenable. Connaughts withdrew under cover of 2nd. Leinsters to the MORCOURT - FRAMERVILLE ridge.) The Battalion conformed to the movements.	
		about 12.30 p.m.	The withdrawal became general along the whole front. As the enemy had pushed through PROYART and were moving up the MORCOURT Rd. "C" Coy under Capt McCann(M.G.) was moved to position on the ridge ¾ mile W of PROYART to prevent the enemy forcing a wedge between 47th. & 48th. BDE. THE general line of withdrawal appeared to be S.W. In the direction of LA -MOTTE - ESTREES Rd. "C" Coy with the assistance of a small party of Hants delayed the enemy advance causing them severe casualties and withdrew fighting a rear-guard action during the afternoon till it reached the Wood ⅝ mile S.W. of MORCOURT where they dug in for the night facing MORCOURT and threw out outposts. Capt. McCann (M.G.) was severely wounded on this position. Capt. Webster's Coy moved parallel with the main LA-MOTTE Rd Keeping about ½ mile to the N taking up several positions and delaying the advance of the enemy.	
		about 5 p.m.	Capt. Webster's was ordered to place his left on the Wood about ⅝ mile N of LA-MOTTE and form the left flank of a line extending past BAYON VILLERS. On arrival at the Wood the enemy were found in possession and the Company withdrew S across the LA-MOTTE Rd where they dug in for the night about 800 yards on a line running S facing W as the enemy were in LA MOTTE. At dawn 28th. the Company cut its way through to VILLERS BRETTONEUX.	
	28/3/18	6 a.m.	"C" Coy who had now come under the orders of Capt. H.Goodland of Munsters Fusiliers with a detachment of 2 Coys R.M.F. 3 Officers & about 40 O.Rs. of the R.Dublin Fusiliers and a few R.Es and other men occupied the high ground, the left of the line lying on the Wood, and the right supposed to be covered by the Gloucester Regt who however could not be located.	

WAR DIARY
or
INTELLIGENCE SUMMARY.

(Erase heading not required.)

Army Form C. 2118.

Place	Date	Hour	Summary of Events and Information	Remarks and references to Appendices
			Picquets were thrown out on the left (into the edge of the wood) from the centre and on the right. Before dark came down the enemy appeared to be gathering on the opposite side of the valley and the line was subjected to heavy M.G. Fire as well as Shell Fire. Several Casualties occured and Capt. McCann (M.C.) 2nd. Leinster Regt. was wounded about dusk. During the night Capt. Goodland reported his position to O.C. 1st. R.M.F. and the Bde. Major 47th. I.Bde and received orders to withdraw his force at dawn as it seemed nearly surrounded to a position lining the road from BAYON - VILLIERS to MORCOURT, with his left lying on the main road and facing N.W. with a view of joining in the counter-attack which would be launched at dawn by the 61st. Division from West of LA MOTTE. The move was affected in good order and at daylight the line was subjected to heavy M.G. Fire from the large wood mentioned above, and the counter-attack as expected did not materialized. It became necessary on account of heavy casualties to withdraw the right of the line,which was done, under cover of our L.G.fire, and at 10 O'clock orders were received from O.C. 1st R.M.F. to withdraw this force to the S. of the Main Road. This was done in good order under cover of our L.Gs. The party appeared to get seperated at this point, 1 party of R.M.F. going to CAIX under order's of O.C. 1st. R.M.Fs. and the remainder of "C" Coy 2nd. Leinster Regt. under the R.S.M. going to MARCEL - CAVE where he came into action again with some of the 39th. Division. Eventually most of the party reached BOVES and rejoined their Bde at AUBIGNY on the 29th. inst.	
	30/3/18.		Battalion in Billets at AUBIGNY.	
	31/3/18.		Battalion in Billets at AUBIGNY.	
			Casualties in Officer's during operations 27th.- 29th.	
			Wounded. Capt. Webster,Capt. McCann (M.C.) Capt. Farrell.	
			Missing. 2/Lt.Spencer,2/Lt. Miller,2/Lieut. Snook, 2/Lieut. Holmes.	

Lieut. Colonel.
Commanding 2nd. Battalion Leinster Regiment

CONFIDENTIAL.

WAR   DIARY

CONFIDENTIAL.

WAR DIARY

of

2nd Battalion, Leinster Regiment.

From 1st April, 1918 To 30th April, 1918.

(VOLUME NO. 1).

WAR DIARY
INTELLIGENCE SUMMARY

(Erase heading not required.)

2nd Leinster Regiment.

Army Form C.2118.

Instructions regarding War Diaries and Intelligence Summaries are contained in F.S. Regs., Part II. and the Staff Manual respectively. Title pages will be prepared in manuscript.

Place	Date	Hour	Summary of Events and Information	Remarks and references to Appendices
FIELD	APRIL, 1st.		Battalion in billets AUDIGNY re-organising.	
	2nd.		Battalion proceeded to HAMLET as Brigade supports under Capt. Goodland (R.M.F.) at 12 a.m. on arrival Lieut. Col. H.W.Weldon took command. The village was shelled at intervals and we lost one man killed and two wounded.	
	3rd.		Brigade supports at Hamlet until relieved at 3-15 p.m. by a Brigade of the 14th. Division when the Battalion proceeded on foot for about 8 Kilos. where lorries were waiting to take Battalion on to SALLEUX where A arrived about 10 p.m. and billetted for the night. Battalion marched to SALLEUX Station at 3 p.m. and entrained at 1-30 a.m. the following day for BLANGY.	
	4th.			
	5th.		Battalion arrived at BLANGY Station about 8 a.m. and proceeded to BOUILLANCOURT where the Battalion billetted.	
	6th.		Battalion in billets at BOUILLANCOURT. Day devoted to general cleaning up, except for Commanding Officers' Parade 11 a.m. to 12 noon.	
	7th.		Battalion at BOUILLANCOURT (Sunday). Divine Service in local church for R.C.'s at 10 a.m. same hour for C of E at LETRANSLAY. Battalion were paid.	
	8th.		Battalion at BOUILLANCOURT, parades under Company arrangements and C.O.'s parade at 11 a.m. until 12 noon. Six Officers and one hundred and thirty O.R.'s joined the Bn. from the 16th. Entrenching Battalion.	
	9th.		Battalion left BOUILLANCOURT for St. QUENTIN at 9 a.m. and arrived at St. QUENTIN 3-15 p.m. and billetted the night.	
	10th.		Battalion marched to EU Station and entrained for ARQUES arrived at ARQUES 4 p.m. Battalion marched to HEURINGHEN and billetted for the night.	
	11th.		Battalion left HEURINGHEN at 10 a.m. and marched to THIEMBRONNE and arrived at 5 p.m. where the Bn. billetted.	
	12th.		Battalion at THIEMBRONNE, day devoted to Company re-organising, the double company into four single companys, with four platoons each. Capt. J.A.J.Farrell rejoined the Battalion as second in command and Capt. G.F.Greville rejoined and took over command "D" Company.	
	13th.		Battalion at THIEMBRONNE, parades from 11-30 a.m. to 12-30 p.m. The Battalion received orders at 1 p.m. to move from THIEMBRONNE and to be at a place south of DRION-VILLE at 2-45 p.m. The Battalion took on the strength four platoons of the 6th. Connaught Rangers, one platoon for each Company. The Battalion then moved off, "D" Coy. at WISMES, "A" Coy. at FORDEECQUES B.n.d billetted for the night. Headquarters and "A" Coy. at WISMES, "D" Coy at FORDEECQUES, B.n.d and billetted for the night. C & D Coy at St. Pione.	

Army Form C.2118.

WAR DIARY
INTELLIGENCE SUMMARY.
(Erase heading not required)

2nd Leinster Regiment.

Instructions regarding War Diaries and Intelligence
Summaries are contained in F. S. Regs., Part II.
and the Staff Manual respectively. Title pages
will be prepared in manuscript.

Place	Date	Hour	Summary of Events and Information	Remarks and references to Appendices
FIELD	APRIL 14th.		The Battalion received orders to move to DELETTE outside HALTE-DOUVRE where the Battalion completed defiolences as far as possible from the 6th. Connaught Rangers. At 2-45 p.m. the Battalion resumed their march to DELETTE whereathey arrived at 4-30 p.m. and billetted for the night.	
	15th.		The Battalion marched from DELETTE to STEENBECQUE, halted mid-day for dinner and arrived STEENBECQUE at 5 p.m. where the Battalion bivouced for the night.	
	16th.		The Battalion at STEENBECQUE; Parades:- digging line of trenches South of MORBECQUE. A draft of 68 O.R.'s arrived and were taken on the strength.	
	17th.		The Battalion at STEENBECQUE- parades the same as previous day.	
	18th.		" " " " " " " "	
	19th.		" " " " " " " "	
	20th.		" " " " " " " "	
	21st.		" " " C of E & R C. Divine Service in the morning and continuation of work on the trenches in the afternoon.	
	22nd.		The Battalion at STEENBECQUE- Work continued.	
	23rd.		The Battalion left STEENBECQUE at 8-15 a.m. by marce route to join 28th. Division near HONDEGHEM where we were pented to the 85th. Brigade. The Battalion were under canvas.	
	24th.		The Battalion under canvas near HONDEGHEM- day devoted to general clean up &colouring tents.	
	25th.		The Battalion moved from HONDEGHEM to a spot S.W. of the BOIS DES HUIT RUES- near SERCUS where the camp was pitched. In the evening diagram maps of the XV Corps Defence works were distributed to Officers. Notice had been given that we were going up the Line very soon.	
	26th.		The Battalion fell in at 6-30 a.m. and proceeded to SWARTENBROUCK where trenches were dug. Company Commanders, Signalling & Intelligence Officers went and reconnoitered the assembly places. Major Frend & Lt. Rebb reconnoitered the forward positions and front line where Battalion was going shortly. During the day the working party suffered a few casualties-one of which was caused by H.E. shrapnel, others due to Gas.	
	27th.		The Battalion got orders to move into the front line opposite VIEUX BERQUIN. Leading Company marched off at 5-30 p.m. During the relief the enemy shelled the road from Brigade H.Q. and caught some of our men in its M.G. fire. The Battalion suffered numerous casualties, two Officers were wounded viz; 2/Lieut. Maguire - killed. 2/Lieut. Thackly wounded, number of other ranks wounded or killed unknown as yet. Battalion relieved the 10th. EAST YORKSFIRE Regt. - relief complete at 1-20 a.m. Major. Frend is commanding the Battalion	

Army Form C. 2118.

WAR DIARY
INTELLIGENCE SUMMARY.
(Erase heading not required.)

2nd Leinster Regiment.

Place	Date	Hour	Summary of Events and Information	Remarks and references to Appendices
FIELD.	APRIL 28th.		The night passed quietly.- Early this morning Lieut. Col. Welden came up to Battalion Hd. Qrs. and conferred with Major. Frend. During the afternoon Bge. General Jackson visited Battalion H.Q. - About 10 P.M. Capt. Plewman, Lieut. Thornley, & 2/Lieut. Toher were accidently wounded - some of "B" Coy men were wounded by shell fire. About midnight Bde. General Freyberg visited Battalion H.Qrs. and went round the line.	
	29th.		This morning news that Capt. Plewman died during the early hours of the morning. About 10 a.m. the Brigadier and C.O. of the S.W.B. went round the line and informed us that we are taking over the portion of the reserve line they held at present.- Major Frend reconnoitered the new position.	
	30th.		Lieut. Col. Welden visited the Battalion Hd. Qrs. and went round "D" Company's new line. The C.O. of the S.W.B. visited Bn. Hd. Qrs. and informed us he is going to relieve the Battalion at the end of our tour. In the evening Major Frend - Medical Officer & Padre went round the line - During the tour the doctor fell into a river.	

Walter Frend

Commanding 2nd Battn., Leinster Regiment.

CONFIDENTIAL

WAR DIARY

of

2nd Battalion, Leinster Regiment.

From 1st May, 1918. To 31st May, 1918.

(VOLUME NO. 2).

Army Form C. 2118.

WAR DIARY
or
INTELLIGENCE SUMMARY
(Erase heading not required.)

Instructions regarding War Diaries and Intelligence Summaries are contained in F. S. Regs., Part II. and the Staff Manual respectively. Title Pages will be prepared in manuscript.

Place	Date	Hour	Summary of Events and Information	Remarks and references to Appendices
FIELD	MAY 1st.		Battalion in Front Line Trenches, Left Sector Divisional Front (under orders 87th. Inf. Bde.) G.O.C. 88th. Inf. Brigade made a tour of the line - a quiet day.	
	2nd.		Battalion relieved by 2nd. S.W.Bs. in the Line and proceeded to Brigade Reserve in billets.	
	3rd.		During afternoon enemy shelled our billets with H.E.& Gas Shells, the Battalion suffered 28 casualties (15 wounded & 13 Gassed) including 2/Lieut. Conlon (Gassed-).	
	4th.		Battalion in Reserve to 87th. Inf. Brigade. Nothing of interest to report.	
	5th.		The 88th. Inf. Brigade relieved 87th. Inf. Brigade in left Sector, the Battalion remained in Brigade Reserve coming under the orders of G.O.C. 88th. Inf. Brigade.	
	6th.		A quiet day.- Battalion found working parties of 350 Other Ranks.	
	7th.		"D" Coy relieved "A" Coy of 4th. Worcestershire Regt. in support.(Pt. SEC. BOTTS) .2/Lieut Jinks joined Battalion from Base. Working parties as on 6th. inst.	
	8th.		A quiet day. Working parties as on 6th. inst.	
	9th.		Change of Brigade boundary, causing a re-disposition of Brigade- "D" Coy. returned to former billets in E.8.a.	
	10th.		Capt. A.H.Whitehead resumed duties of Adjutant on return from Hospital - Battalion Hd. Qrs. was transferred to E.7.d.7.7. -working parties as usual. Major B.J.Jones joined the Battalion from Base.	
	11th.		Battalion in Brigade Reserve, day passed quietly, - at night billets were shelled with Gas & 10 casualties caused in "B" Coy. by a shell bursting in a billet.	
	12th.		Battalion in Brigade Reserve - Competition for best turned out soldier at Transport Lines. Battalion Hd. Qrs. were shelled with 4-2s during evening, no casualties.	
	13th.		Battalion relieved by 2nd. S.W.Bs. & Marched to Camp at Gd. HASARD - a good relief.	
	14th.		Battalion found 390 men for working parties on support and reserve positions of Right Sector. Enemy planes passed over Camp at night, no bombs were dropped near Camp.	
	15th.& 16th.		In camp at Gd. HASARD.- Working parties as on 14th. inst. Remainder of Battalion training. A lecture & demonstration in use of Rifle Grenades No.36. given.	
	17th.		Working parties as usual. Inter-Battalion sports with 4th. Worcestershire Regt. in evening which the Battalion won 5 events to 3.	
	18th.		A draft of 179 other ranks from Base arrived & accomodated at Transport Lines. 2/Lieut. J.J.Barry (Connaught Rangers) joined for duty. Working parties as usual.	
	19th.		The Battalion relieved 3 Coys. 1st. R.D.F. & 2 Coys. Lancs. Fus. in Front Line Right Sector (see attached Operation Orders No.6.) I.O.R. killed , 3 wounded during relief.	
	20th.		At 4 p.m. the Battalion on our right carried out an enterprise with the object of advancing their line which was successful.- Enemy shelled our Right Coy. who had 1 Killed & 4 Wounded.	

2449 Wt. W14957/M90 750,000 1/16 J.B.C. & A. Forms/C.2118/12.

Army Form C. 2118.

WAR DIARY
or
INTELLIGENCE SUMMARY
(Erase heading not required.)

Instructions regarding War Diaries and Intelligence Summaries are contained in F.S. Regs., Part II. and the Staff Manual respectively. Title Pages will be prepared in manuscript.

Place	Date	Hour	Summary of Events and Information	Remarks and references to Appendices
FIELD.	MAY 21st.		At 3 a.m. enemy attempted to retake ground lost on 20th. but failed - A heavy barrage was put down on our line but our casualties were slight.	
	22nd.		Early the enemy shelled our positions heavily in response to our Raid. "B" Coy. suffered 20 casualties from the heavy Gas bombardment.	
	23rd.		A patrol reported (at midnight) considerable enemy movements towards VERT RUE, a relief being suspected. Brigade informed and artillery fired on the point.	
	23rd.		Battalion relived in the line by 4th. Worcestshire Regt. & moved into Brigade Reserve near MORBECQUE (D.2.o.6.) Total casualties during 4 days were 3 Killed, 2 Died of Wounds, 41 Wounded & Gassed (including Capt. Staniforth, 2/Lieut. Slowey, 2/Lieut Chapman gassed & evacuated)	
	24th.		Assembly positions & defences of LA MOTTE reconnitred by all officers. - A quiet day. Information communicated to officers that an attack is expected on our front between 25th. & 28th. Inst.	
	25th.		A wet day, troops resting in Camp.	
	26th.		In Camp- Bands of 29th. Division & 2nd. Hants. Regt. played during afternoon & evening.	
	27th.		The Battalion relieved 2 Coys. of 2nd. Hants. Regt. & 2 Coys. Worcestershire Regt. in Support Positions, Right Sector with Hd. Qrs. at E.24.c.7. (Operation Orders attached) A good relief, complete at 10-30 p.m. A message received at 11 p.m. from Brigade that an attack by the enemy was expected in the early morning. The Battalion stood to Arms & Major. Frend and the Adjutant made a tour of all positions.	
	28th.		Unusually quiet day. Battalion found 510 Other Ranks for working parties.	
	29th.		A quiet day. Leave re-opened.	
	30th.		Early in morning enemy shelled positions occupied by "D" Coy. & LA MOTTE causing casualties, 2 O.R. Killed, 11 Wounded.	
	31st.		Battalion relieved by 4th. Worcestershire Regt. in support & relieved the 2 Hants. Regt. in Front Line (see Operation Orders No.9.) relief complete 12-15 a.m. on 1st. June. A good relief.	

6.6.1918.

[signature]
Lieut. Colonel.
Commanding 2nd. Battn. The Leinster Regiment.

OPERATION ORDERS. No. 6
By
Lieut. Col. H. W. Welden.   COPY   No. 3
Commanding 2nd. Battn. The Leinster Regt.

In the Field.   19th. May. 1918.

(1) The Battalion will relieve 3 Companies of the 1st. Royal Dublin
    Fusiliers & 2 Companies of Lancashire Fusiliers in the Right Sector on
    night May 19/20.

(2) On completion the Battalion will be disposed as follows:-
    FRONT LINE (LEFT) - "C" COY. (relieving "W" COY. R.D. Fusiliers)
    "   "   (RIGHT)- "D" COY. ("   "X" COY. R.D. Fusiliers)
    SUPPORT   (LEFT) - "A" COY. ("   "Y" COY. R.D. Fusiliers)
    "   "   (RIGHT)- "B" COY. ("   "A" & "D" COY. LANCS. ")
    BATTALION HEADQUARTERS at E.14.c.8.o.

(3) ROUTE:- From Railway D.15.b.4.1. via Cross-Country track to
    PAPOTE - le MOTTE Road at D.23.a.2.3. Thence along road to direct Ride
    to D.30. b.5.4. thence by cross-country track to SAW MILLS.
    Battalion Scouts will be posted along route at important points.

(4) GUIDES:- 4 per company & 1 for Company Headquarters from R.D.F. &
    Lancs. Fusiliers will be at SAW MILLS E.19.d.2.1. (No guides for H.Q.Coy)
    as follows:-
         For "B" COY. (from LANCS FUS.) at 7 p.m.
         "   "A" COY. ("   R.D.F.   ) at 7-15 p.m.
         " C & D COY ("   R.D.F.   ) at 8 p.m.
    Companies will parade 1½ hours before their time.

(5) ADVANCE PARTIES. of 1 Officer, 1 N.C.O. & 1 Runner per Company & 1
    Officer (Battn. Intelligence Officer) 1 N.C.O. & 2 Runners from
    Headquarters will leave Camp at 11 a.m. and proceed to take over.
    The runners will ascertain locations of Battalion H.Qrs. & all
    Company Headquarters.
    Trench Store Lists to be at ORDERLY ROOM by 10 a.m. 20th. inst.

(6) All packs and stores for Transport Lines to be ready stacked at NORTH
    ENTRANCE to Camp at 10 a.m.
    Officers surplus Kits, Mess Gear not required for line, ready at 2 p.m.
    Mess Kits etc., for Line ready at 5-30 p.m.

(7) The present Camp will be handed over to Unit of 86th. Brigade by Q.M.
    All Lines to be left in a perfectly clean condition and certificates
    rendered from Companies to this effect.

(8) Relief to be reported complete by all Companies to Battn. Hd. Qrs. by
    code message "NEAR CLASSIC"

                              (sd)   A.H. WHITEHEAD.   Capt.
                              Adjt. 2nd. Battn. The Leinster Regiment.

DISTRIBUTION.

COPY. 1. C.O.   COPY. 9. O.C. "B" COY.
  "   2. 2nd. in Command.   "   10. O.C. "C" COY.
  "   3. Adjutant.   "   11. O.C. "D" COY.
  "   4. Signalling Officer.   "   12. 88th. Infantry Brigade.
  "   5. Intelligence   "   "   13. 1st. R.D.F.
  "   6. Quartermaster.   "   14. Lancashire Fusiliers.
  "   7. Transport Officer.   "   15. R.S.M.
  "   8. O.C. "A" COY.   "   16. W A R   D I A R Y.
                                    "   17. F I L E.

SECRET   COPY No. 8

OPERATION ORDER No. 8.

By Lt-Colonel H.W. WELDON., Commanding 2nd. Bn. Leinster Regt

In the Field   26th May, 1918.

1. The Battalion will relieve 2 Companies of the 2nd Hants Regiment and 1 Company and 2 Platoons of the 4th Worcestershire Regiment in the Support positions, Right Sector, on night of 27/28th May, 1918.

2. On completion the disposition of the Battalion will be as follows:-

   "A" Coy. 3 Platoons in E.20.Central relieving 2 Platoons 4th Worcesters.
   "A" Coy. 1 Platoon BOURRE RIVER posts relieving 1 Platoon 2nd Hants.
   "B" Coy. (Less 1.L.G.Sectn)SWARTENBROUGH relieving 1 Coy.4th Worcesters.
   "C" Coy. (Less 2 L.G.Sectns)Reserve Line.E.19.c.relieving 1 Coy 2nd Hants.
   "D" Coy. (Less 1.L.G.Sectn)LA MOTTE SWITCH relieving 3 Platoons 2nd Hants.
   (1 Platoon of "A" Coy and 4 Lewis Gun Sections in BOURRE River posts will be under Command of 2/Lieut W.H. Barker).
   Battalion Headquarters at E.24.a.7.1.

3. GUIDES (1 per Platoon and 1 for Coy.H.Q.) will meet incoming units as follows :-

   "A" Coy. (E.20.Central)at SAW MILLS, E.19.d.1.1. at 4 P.M. from Worcs.
   "A" Coy. (BOURRE RIVER)at SAW MILLS, E.19.d.1.1. at 4 P.M. from Hants.
   "B" Coy. (SWARTENBROUGH)at X.Roads, E.19.b.7.8. at 9 P.M. from Worcs.
   "C" Coy. (E.19.c.)   at SAW MILLS, E.19.d.1.1. at 4 P.M. from Hants.
   "D" Coy. (LA MOTTE SWITCH)End of Track D.30.a.4.5. at 4 P.M.from Hants.

4. ADVANCE PARTIES - 1 Officer 1 N.C.O and 1 Runner per Company (1 Officer 1 N.C.O. and 2 Runners from Headquarters) will leave Camp at 11 A.M. and proceed to take over.

5. Copies of Local Defence Schemes, Maps Areo-photos and Trench Stores will be taken over. Receipts to be at Orderly Room by 10 A.M. 27th.

6. TRANSPORT. 1 Limber each for A. C. and D. Coys and 1 for party for BOURRE River to be at Camp at 2.30 P.M. 1 Limber for "B" Coy at 7.30.PM Mess Cart, Maltese Cart and 1 Limber for Headquarters at 3 P.M.

7. The Quartermaster will hand over present Camp to advance party of incoming unit. All lines and Barns to be left in a clean state and certificates to this effect handed to Adjutant.

8. Completion of relief to be reported to Battalion Headquarters by Code Message - "BLACK LABEL".

                                        (S'd) A. H. Whitehead. Captain & Adjutant
                                              2nd Battalion The Leinster Regiment.

DISTRIBUTION

Copy No. 1. Commanding Officer.   Copy No. 9. Quartermaster
         2. 2nd in Command.   10. Signalling Office
         3. Adjutant.   11. Intelligence Offr
         4. O.C.,"A" Company.   12. Regt Sergt Major
         5. O.C.,"B" Company.   13. 88th Infantry Bde
         6. O.C.,"C" Company.   14. 4th Worcester Reg
         7. O.C.,"D" Company.   15. 2nd Hants Regt.
         8. Transport Officer.   16. File.

SECRET.   COPY NO......

OPERATION ORDER NO. 9

By Lieut-Colonel H. W. WELDON, Commanding 2nd Leinster Regt.

Ref Map Sheet 36A N.E.(Edn 7) 1/20,000.   30th May, 1918.

1. The Battn will be relieved in Support Positions of the Right Sector on the night 31st May/June 1st by the 4th Worcestershire Regt, and on completion will relieve the 2nd Hampshire Regt in the Front Line.

2. On completion, the disposition of Battn will be as follows:

        Front Line (Left) "A" Coy relieving "X" Coy, 2nd Hampshire R.
           do.   (Right)"B"   "   " "Z" "   "   "   "
        Support Line (Left) "C"   "   " "Y" "   "   "   "
           do.   (Right)"D"   "   " "W" "   "   "   "
        Battn H.Q. at E.14.c.9.0.

3. Guides to meet incoming Unit (4th Worcestershire Regt) - one per platoon and one per Coy H.Q. - will be found as follows:

   (a) By "A" Coy (E.20.Central & BOURRE River) SAWMILLS at 6 p.m.
          "B" " (SWARTENBROUCK) at X Roads E.19.b.9.5. at 9 p.m.
          "C" " (Reserve Line) end of Track D.30.a.4.5. at 5.15 p.m.
          "D" " (LA MOTTE Switch) end of Track D.30.a.4.5. at 5.30 p.m.

   (b) Guides from 2nd Hampshire Regt will meet 2nd Leinster Coys as follows:

          "A" Coy R.E. Dump E.20.?.?.0. at 9 p.m.
          "B" "   do.   do.   at 9.30 p.m.
          "C" " SAW MILLS at 6 p.m.
          "D" "   do.   at 6.30 p.m.

4. Advance parties as usual will proceed at 4 p.m. to take over Defence Schemes, Work policies, Trench Stores. Lists to be returned to Battn H.Q. by 10 a.m. 1st June.

5. <u>Transport.</u> A limber will collect cooking utensils from Coys at 5 p.m. and dump them at E.20.c.2.6. Mess Cart and Maltese cart to be at present Battn H.Q. at 8 p.m.

6. Completion of Relief by 4th Worcestershire Regt to be reported to present Battn H.Q. by Code message "J WALKER". Completion of Relief of 2nd Hampshire Regt to be reported to new H.Q. by Code message "THREE STARS".

                                          [signature]
                                          Captain & Adjutant,
                                          2nd Leinster Regiment.

DISTRIBUTION:-

    1 C.O.   7 Rear H.Q.
    2 Adjutant   8 88th Inf. Bde.
    3 O.C. "A" Coy.   9 4th Worc. R.
    4 O.C. "B" "   10 2nd Hamps. R.
    5 O.C. "C" "   11 R. S. M.
    6 O.C. "D" "   12 File.

CONFIDENTIAL

WAR DIARY

OF

2nd Battalion, The Leinster Regiment.

From 1st June, 1918   To 30th June, 1918.

(VOLUME NO. 3)

CONFIDENTIAL

29th Division No. 317/14

D.A.G.,
    Base.

    War Diary of 2nd Bn. Leinster Regt. for the month of June is forwarded herewith reference your No. 8700/1630 of 19-8-18.

24th August, 1918.

Brigadier-General
Commanding 29th Division.

Army Form C. 2118.

WAR DIARY of 2nd Lincs.
INTELLIGENCE SUMMARY
(Erase heading not required.)

Instructions regarding War Diaries and Intelligence
Summaries are contained in F. S. Regs., Part II.
and the Staff Manual respectively. Title pages
will be prepared in manuscript.

Place	Date	Hour	Summary of Events and Information	Remarks and references to Appendices
In the Field.	June 1st.		Battalion in Right Sector Front Line. — Quiet day.	
	2nd.		Battalion in Right Sector Front Line. "C" Coy advanced the line by digging 3 new posts	
			on the SEHGIN - LUG FARM LINE, in conjunction with an attack by the Left Brigade on LUG FARM	
	3rd.		Battalion in Right Section Front Line. - Quiet day.	
	4th.		Battalion was relieved by the BORDER Regt. in the Front Line. On completion of relief the	
			Battalion marched to Camp at D.15. in Divisional Reserve.	
	5th.		Battalion in Divisional Reserve.	
	6th.		Battalion moved Camp to D.7.a.	
	7th.& 8th.		Battalion in Divisional Reserve.	
	9th.		Battalion paraded for Divine Service at 9-30 a.m. Major. General Cayley, G.O.C. 29th.	
			Division, visited the Commanding Officer in the afternoon.	
	10th.		"B" & "D" Coys. supplied 300 men at 9 a.m. for work on the FOURRE POSTS. "A" & "C" supplied	
			300 men in the evening for the same task. The Corps Gas Officer gave a Lecture in the	
			afternoon, which was attended by the Officers and N.C.Os. of the Battalion.	
			Lieut. N. F. Hamilton and 2/Lieut. A. J. Ward joined the Battalion from the Base.	
	11th.		The Battalion relieved the 1st. Lancs. Fusiliers with A, B, and D Coys in Brigade Reserve	
			Left Sector. Operation Orders attached. "C" Coy was attached to 2nd. Hants. and joined them	
			on relief. Companies were disposed of as per para. 2 of O.O	

WAR DIARY INTELLIGENCE SUMMARY

(Erase heading not required.)

Army Form C.2118.

Instructions regarding War Diaries and Intelligence Summaries are contained in F.S. Regs., Part II. and the Staff Manual respectively. Title pages will be prepared in manuscript.

Place	Date	Hour	Summary of Events and Information	Remarks and references to Appendices
In the Field.	June 12th.		Battalion less "C" Coy in Brigade Reserve, Left Sector. - Quiet Day.	
			"C" Coy. took up Support Line from SANITAS CORNER TO CO'LERY COTTAGE.	
	13th.		Battalion in Brigade Reserve Left Sector. - Quiet Day. Major. Jones. D.S.O. left for the 2nd. Royal Inniskilling Fusiliers. Lieut. N.V.Hamilton wounded.	
	14th.		Battalion in Brigade Reserve - Quiet Day. "C" Coy. was relieved in Support Line by 2nd. Hunts and took up position in L. Line. C.H.Q. Le BOULEVARD. Lieut. White joined the Battalion.	
	15th.		Battalion in Brigade Reserve. LUG, ANKLE, and FANTASY FARMS taken by the enemy. 2/d. Hunts. regained FANTASY FARM. "C" Coy moved up into Support Line in front of PETIT-SEC-BOIS.	
	16th.		Battalion in Brigade Reserve. - Quiet Day. Lieut. J.H. de G. MacDonald gassed.	
	17th.		The Battalion relieved the 2nd. Hunts in the Front Line Subsection, Left Sector. Operation Orders attached. 2/Lieut Crowley joined the Battalion from Base. 2/Lieut. Morrison rejoined from Hospital.	
	18th.		Battalion in Right Subsection, Left Sector Front Line. - Quiet Day.	
	19th.	At 12-45 a.m.	"A" Coy. Attacked and captured LUG F.M. with heavy Artillery barrage. 2 Machine Guns and 1 Wounded Bosche were taken. 2/Lieut.A.J.Ward Killed. Casualties 1 O.R. Killed 40 wounded. "B" Company relieved "A" Coy. in Front Line at night. Major.J.R. Frend D.S.O. in Command.	

Army Form C. 2118.

WAR DIARY *2nd Leinster Regt*
or
INTELLIGENCE SUMMARY.

(Erase heading not required.)

Instructions regarding War Diaries and Intelligence Summaries are contained in F. S. Regs., Part II. and the Staff Manual respectively. Title pages will be prepared in manuscript.

Place	Date	Hour	Summary of Events and Information	Remarks and references to Appendices
In the Field.	June 20th.		Lieut.General De Lisle visits the Support Line. - The Battalion was relieved in the Front Line; Right Subsection; Left Sector Front Line by the 13th. Yorks and Lancs. Operation Orders attached. - On completion the Battalion marched to Camp outside LA KREULE.	
	21st.		Battalion in Corps Reserve.- At 5-30 p.m. the Battalion entrained at BOWDEGEM for LUMBRES. On arrival, the Battalion encamped at VAL DE LUMBRES. Adjutant went to Hospital. The following Officers joined from the Base:- Lieut. S.A.McNeill, 2/Lieut. L.J.Hutchinson, 2/Lieut. V.A.Davis, 2/Lieut. G.Smith, 2/Lieut. D.O'C.Fitzsimons, 2/Lieut. B.N. Midgeley, 2/Lieut. Scott J., 2/Lieut. J.J.Igoe.	
	22nd.		The Battalion cleaning up.	
	23rd.		The Battalion paraded for Divine Service; R.Cs. at LUMBRES CHURCH at 9 a.m. C.of Es. Service in Camp at 11-30 a.m. Lieut. General De LISLE attended the C.of Es. service afterwards inspected the Parade.	
	24th. to 29th.		Company Parades.	
	30th.		The Battalion paraded for Divine Service as follows; R.Cs. at LUMBRES CHURCH at 9 a.m. C.of Es. at 11-30 a.m. in Camp. General Plumer, Commanding 2nd. Army, attended the C.of Es. Service and afterwards inspected the Parade.	

J. R. Hunt. Major.
Commanding 2nd. Battalion Leinster Regiment.

SECRET.
OPERATION ORDERS No. 7
by
Lieut. Col. E.W.Weldon.   C O P Y No. ....
Commanding 2nd. Battn. Leinster Regt.

Ref. Map Sheet 36A N.E. (E.d.7)
                                                                    11.6.1918.

1. On night 11/12 June, A, B & D Coys will relieve the 1st Lancs.
   Fusiliers in Brigade Reserve, Left Sector.
   At same time "C" Coy. will be attached to 2nd. Hants. Regt & will
   join them in Camp at D.20.b.

2. On completion the disposition of Battalion will be as follows:-
   "A" Coy. Billets E.7.b.4.0.
   "B" Coy 2 Platoons Trenches E.7.a. & 2 Platoons Reserve E.13.d. &
   D.14.a.
   "D" Coy. Billets D.12.a.3.1.
   "C" Coy. Camp at D.20.b. (attached 2nd. Hants)
   Battalion Hd. Qrs. E8.d.85.75.

3. Guides will meet Companys as follows:-
   "A" Coy (from "B" Coy. 1st. Lancs Fus.) at "HALT" D.11.b.0.1. at 7 p.m.
   "B" Coy.(" " D" Coy.   "   " 2 Platoons at "HALT"   at 8 p.m.
                                         2 Platoons at M.13.c.3.7.   at 8 p.m.
   "D" Coy. Battn. Hd. Qrs. at "HALT" D.11.b.e.1. at 8 p.m.
   Companies will march out of camp 1½ hours before these times, "D" Coy at
   4-30 p.m.

4. All Packs, Officers Kits & Mess gear to be returned to Transport Lines
   will be stacked on lane-way at 2 p.m.

5. Trench Stores, Defence Schemes, Air Photos? A.A. Mountings & Positions will
   be taken over.   Lists to be at Orderly Room by 10 a.m. 12th. inst.

6. Present Camp will be left in a scrupulously clean state & handed over
   to incoming unit by Quartermaster.

7. Completion of relief to be reported to Battn Hd. Qrs. by Code Message
   "TAWNY".

                                                  Whitehead
                                                         Capt.
                                        Adjt. 2nd. Battn. Leinster Regiment.

D I S T R I B U T I O N.
C O P Y.   1.   O.O.
  "   2.   2nd. in Command.
  "   3.   Adjutant.
  "   4.   Signalling Officer.
  "   5.   Quartermaster.
  "   6.   Transport Officer.
  "   7.   O.C. "A" Coy.
  "   8.   O.C. "B" Coy.
  "   9.   O.C. "C" Coy.
  "   10.   O.C. "D" Coy.
  "   11.   88th. Infantry Brigade.
  "   12.   1st. Lancs. Fusiliers.
  "   13.   War Dairy.
  "   14.   File.
  "   15.   R.S.M.

CONFIDENTIAL.

WAR DIARY

of

2nd Battalion The Leinster Regiment.

From 1st July, 1918.   To 31st July, 1918.

(Volume No. 4).

WAR DIARY or INTELLIGENCE SUMMARY

Army Form C. 2118.

2nd. Battalion Leinster Regt.

JULY 1918.

Place	Date	Hour	Summary of Events and Information	Remarks and references to Appendices
In the Field LUMBRES	1st.		Major General Cayley, G.O.C., 29th. Division inspected the 88th. Brigade at 11 a.m. He distributed the following Honours and Awards -	
			Bar to M.C. — Capt. V.J.Farrell M.C.	
			Card of Honour. — 2/Lieut. C.A.N.Holden.	
			" " — 2/Lieut. S.O'C.Mullins.	
			L.G.M. — R.S.M. R. Knight.	
			Bar to M.M. — Pte. M. Byrne. M.M.	
			M.M. — Cpl. W. Jenkins.	
			Card of Honour. — L/C. W. Fitzmaurice.	
			He subsequently expressed himself as highly pleased with the turn-out and parade. Lieut. A.E.NYE & C.T.E.MOORE joined the Battalion from the Base.	
	2nd.		Brigadier General Freyberg V.C.,D.S.O. lunched with Battalion & afterwards judged a Cooker and Guard Mounting Competition. "B" & "C" tied for the first. "C" Coy. won the 2nd.	
	3rd.		Company training.	
	4th.		Company Training. Lieut. J.H. de C. O'C. MacDonald received Card of Honour.	
	5th.		Company Training. The Battalion paraded and marched to School of Musketry Grounds, LUMBRES, where Col. Campbell D.S.O. lectured on "Recreational Training"	
	6th.		Battalion tactical scheme in the morning. 88th. Brigade Sports were held at LUMBRES in the afternoon, when Major. General Cayley attended. The Batjn. won the Tug-of-War, Long Jump, 100 and 330 yards.	
	7th.		The Battalion paraded for Divine Service as follows:- R.C. at Lumbras Church at 9 a.m. C of Es. In Camp at 11.30 a.m. - The Brigade Eliminating Competition for Transport was held, the Battalion winning. The Brigade Eliminating Contest resulted in the Batn.winning the Feather weights, Welter weights and Middle weights.	
	8th.		The Battalion obtained 2 seconds in the Divisional Boxing.	
	9th.		Company Training. The Battalion won the Divisional Transport Competition and the Regtl. Officer's Jumping Contest.	

A6945 Wt. W11422/M1160 350,000 12/16 D.D.&L. Forms/C./2118/14

WAR DIARY
or
INTELLIGENCE SUMMARY.

2nd. LEINSTER REGT.

JULY 1918.

(Erase heading not required.)

Place	Date	Hour	Summary of Events and Information	Remarks and references to Appendices
In the Field.	10th.		The Battalion won the 88th. Brigade open ½ Mile Race, obtaining 1st. and 2nd. place.	
	11th. to 20th.		Battalion in training at LUMBRES. 2/Lieut. W.H.Barker was awarded the M.C.	
	21st.		The Battalion attended Divine Service in Camp as follows:- R.Cs. at 9 a.m., C of Es. 10 a.m.	
(OIELEE)	22nd.		The Battalion marched to BAVINCHOVE where they had dinner. In the afternoon the Battalion encamped at 270 (OXEZAERE AREA) being now in the Xth. Corps.	
	23rd.		No work done.	
	24th.		The Blue Line reconnoitred by Company Officers.	
	25th.			
	26th.		Company Training.	
	27th.			
	28th.		Battalion attended Divine Service as follows:- R.Cs. at CASSEL Church at 11 a.m. C of Es. at 10 a.m. "C" Company held Inter-platoon sports.	
	29th.		Baths.	
	30th.		Company Training.	
	31st.		Company Training.	
	2.8.1918.			

Lieut.Col.
Commanding 2nd. Battalion Leinster Regiment.

CONFIDENTIAL.

WAR DIARY

of

2nd Battalion The Leinster Regiment

From 1st August, 1918 To 31st August, 1918.

(Volume No. 5).

2nd. LEINSTER REGT.
WAR DIARY or INTELLIGENCE SUMMARY.

(Erase heading not required.)

Army Form C. 2118.

Place	Date	Hour	Summary of Events and Information	Remarks and references to Appendices
In the Field.	AUGUST 1st.		Battalion in X Corps Reserve at 27.0.1C.	
	2nd.		Battalion moved at night to XV Corps Reserve at 27 W.8.C. Bn. relieved 7th. Bn. A.I.F. in the line in the MERRIS Sector. The following officers went in:- C.O. Major. J.R. Frend D.S.O., Adjutant, Lieut. A.E. Nye., Signalling Officer 2/Lt. A.N. McMahon. Intelligence Officer 2/Lieut. J. Moran. "A" Company;- 2/Lieut. W.H. Barker, M.C. 2/Lt.V.A. Davis, 2/Lt.C. Smith, 2/Lt.J. Scott. "B" Company;- 2/Lieut. H. Wylde, Lieut.G.W.B. Moore, 2/Lt.L.M.I. Pearson, 2/Lt.J. Ips. "C" Company;- Capt. V.J. Farrell M.C. Lt.R.M. White, 2/Lieut.C.A.N. Holden, 2/Lt.H. Woods, M.M., M.M. "D" Company;- Capt. G.E. Farrell, Lt.F.D.E. Kirkpatrick M.C. 2/Lt. Midgeley, 2/Lt.E.O'Sullivan. A and C Coys took over front line, B Coy Close Support, D Coy Support. Casualties; O.R's. 1 Killed L wounded.— The Battalion TUG-OF-WAR Team beat the A.S.C. in the Final Round of the 2nd. Army Championship.	
	3rd.		Bn. in the line. "A" Coy was relieved by the 12th. Royal Scots in the front line and moved into XX Support. A patrol under 2/Lt.H. Woods M.C. was out. Casualties;- O.R's. 2 Killed, 1wounded.	
	4th.		Bn in the line. A patrol under 2/Lt. C.A.N. Holden was out. Casualties:- O.R's. 7 wounded.	
	5th.		Bn. in the line. A fighting party under Lt. White and 2/Lt. Woods M.C. came in touch with an enemy post. No prisoners could be secured. Casualties;- O.R. 1 wounded.	
	6th.		Bn. in the line. "B" Coy relieved C Coy in the front line. A Coy relieved B Coy in close support. Casualties;- O.R's. 1 killed, 1 wounded.	
	7th.		Bn. in the line. A fighting party under 2/Lt. Midgeley inflicted casualties on the enemy. A patrol under Lt. Kirkpatrick M.C. was also out. Casualties;- 2 O.R's wounded.	
	8th.		Bn. in the line. 2 fighting parties under 2/Lt. Midgeley and O'Sullivan inflicted casualties on the enemy. Casualty - 1 O.R. wounded.	
	9th.		Bn. in the line. 2 daylight patrols were sent out by "D" Coy, under Lt. Kirkpatrick M.C. and 2/Lt. Midgeley. Casualties -nil-.	
	10th.		Bn. in the line. Lt.Col.Weldon returned from leave, and relieved Major. Frend. D.S.O. Capt.J.A.J. Farrell D.S.O. took over Adjutancy from Lt.A.E. Nye. "B" Coy. relieved D.Coy in the front line. A patrol under 2/Lt. Ips.e was out. Casualties;- 3 O.R's killed.	
	11th.		Bn. in the line. The following Other Ranks represented the Battalion on an inspection by H.M. The King;- Pte. R.S.M.H. Knight, D.C.M., C.S.M.O'Brien.M.M., Sergt. Murphy, Sergt. McCarthy, D.C.M., Pte. Byrne M.M., Pte. Pledge.	
	12th.		Bn. in the line. "B" Coy. established and consolidated posts in advance of the front line, meeting with little opposition.	

Army Form C. 2118.

WAR DIARY
or
INTELLIGENCE SUMMARY.
(Erase heading not required.)

Instructions regarding War Diaries and Intelligence Summaries are contained in F. S. Regs., Part II. and the Staff Manual respectively. Title pages will be prepared in manuscript.

Place	Date	Hour	Summary of Events and Information	Remarks and references to Appendices
In the Field.	AUGUST. 12th.		Bn. in the line. The Battalion was relieved by the 1st. K.O.S.B. and moved into Div.sional Reserve at "27.V.23. Casualties:- 2 O.R's wounded.	
	13th.		Bn. in the line. "B" Coy established and consolidated a new post in advance of the front line. Casualties:- 1 O.R. killed, 1 O.R. wounded.	
	15th.		Bn. in Divisional Reserve. Lt. Hitchcock M.C. and Macready M.C. joined from Base.	
	16th.		Bn. in Divisional Reserve.	
	17th.		The Battalion was inspected by Lt.Gen. CHIKUSHI, K.C.M.G., Japanese Army. He afterwards addressed the following letter of thanks and appreciation to Lt.Gen. Sir H. de B. de LISLE, K.C.B., D.S.O., Commanding XVth. Corps:- "It is a great honour to me to have had the privilege of seeing this magnificent belonging to such a famous Division at the 29th. Division. I understand that the Battalion has only just returned from the front line, and its martial appearance, steadiness and turn-out have deeply impressed me. I can only repeat and emphasise my appreciation of having had the honour of inspecting these fine men and beg to thank your Excellency very sincerely. I look forward with ever increasing confidence to final victory."	
	18th.		"D" Coy. supplied 100 men as carrying party to the 1st. K.O.S.B. In the front area. The Battn: moved from 27.V.23. to Reserve Line (from 27.W.21.d. to W.15 central) B.H.Q. at 27.W.20.c.6.8 The following officers went into the line;- C.O. Lt.Col. Weldon, 2nd. in Command. Capt.J.A.J. Farrell D.S.O., Adjutant. Lt. A.E.Nye (relieved by Capt. A.H.Whitehead M.C. on 20th. inst) Intelligence Officer 2/Lt. S. O'C. Mallins. "A" Company:- Lt. Sander, 2/Lt. Shelly, 2/Lt. Davis, Lt. Macready M.C. "B" Company:- 2/Lt. Wylde, Lt. Moore, 2/Lt. Pearson, 2/Lt. Igoe. "C" Company:- Capt.V.J. Parrell M.C., Lt. White, 2/Lt. Fitz-Simon, 2/Lt. Woods.M.C., M.M. "D" Company:- Lt. Kirkpatrick M.C. 2/Lt. J.Moran., 2/Lt. O'Sullivan, 2/Lt. Johnston.	
	19th.		Bn. in Reserve Line.	
	20th.		The Battn. relieved 1st. BORDER Regt in the front line, OUTTERSTEENE Sector.(operation orders attached) C and D Coys. took over the front line, with A and B Coys. in close support. 2 Patrols under 2/Lt. Johnston and 2/Lt. J.Moran were out. Casualties:- 4 O.R's wounded.	
	21st.		Bn. in the front line. Heavy hostile shelling. A daylight patrol under 2/Lt. Fitz-Simon was out. Major J.R. Frend D.S.O. took over command of the 4th. Worcestershire Regt. The front line posts were joined together during the evening. Casualties:- 2/Lt. J.Shelly and Lt. Macready M.C. wounded, O.R's. 1 killed, 3 wounded.	

2nd. LEINSTER REGT.

WAR DIARY
or
INTELLIGENCE SUMMARY.
(Erase heading not required.)

Army Form C. 2118.

Instructions regarding War Diaries and Intelligence Summaries are contained in F.S. Regs., Part II and the Staff Manual respectively. Title pages will be prepared in manuscript.

Place	Date	Hour	Summary of Events and Information	Remarks and references to Appendices
In the Field.	AUGUST. 22nd.		Bn. in the front line. 2/Lt. Moran and 1 O.R. examined DERMOT House.(36A N.E. F.4.) in the afternoon. In the evening, C and D Coys made good the line F.c.6.2.8.-35,85-45,90-F3d.65,25.-7,4, -F4cl5,70-F4a.oo.15-F.3.b.60.25. (Ref. 36 A. NE.) without any casualties to themselves, an advance of approx. 500 yards. Casualties:- 3 killed, 7 O.R's wounded.	
	23rd.		Bn. in the front line. The Battalion was relieved by the 2nd. Hants. and moved into Support. (operation orders attached) B.H.Q. at 27A. 29.d.4.04.20. Companies were disposed of as follows:- Ref. 36A. "A" Coy. F.1.- "B" Coy. 27X26,- "C" Coy. 27.W.29. "D" Coy.-36A NE. E.6. Casualties. -nil-	
	24th.		Battalion in support. Working parties of 5 Officers and 250 Other Ranks were found by the Battalion for work on the front line.	
	25th.		Battalion in support. Working parties of 5 Officers and 200 men were found by the Battalion for work on Support Line. Capt. V.J. Farrell M.C. Commanded the Battalion during the temporary absence of Lt.Col. Weldon.	
	26th.		Bn. in Support. The Battalion was relieved in support by the 1st. K.O.S.B's and took over the "Z" line from the S.W.B's, being attached to the 87th. Inf. Brigade. (Operation Orders attached.- B.H.Q. at 27 W.22.d.90.80.	
	27th.		Bn. in "Z" Line. B,C and D Coys were relieved by a company each of the BORDERS,S.W.B's and K.O.S.B's "A" Company took over the STRAZEELE defences. The remainder of the Battalion moved to Camp in 27 V.23. and came under the orders of the G.O.C. 88th. Inf. Bde.	
	28th.		Bn. less "A" Company in Divisional Reserve. The following letter of appreciation from the C.O. 1st. Bn. K.O.S.B's was published for Information.	

"Dear Colonel,

    The Officers and men of my Battalion have asked me to write and express their great appreciation of the way in which your Battalion, both Officers and men helped us on the night 18/19 August. Without the whole-hearted assistance given us by your Battalion we could never have got up the rations, water and ammunition. If at any time it is in the power of the 1st. K.O.S.B's to do anything to assist the 2nd. Battn. Leinster Regt. I only hope that we shall be able to carry out the assistance as effectually as all ranks of your Battalion did for us on the night 18/19th. August 1918.

Believe me,
Yours most gratefully,
G. E. BEATY-POWNELL,
Commanding 1st. K.O.S.B.

Army Form C. 2118.

2nd Leinster Regt

WAR DIARY
or
INTELLIGENCE SUMMARY.
(Erase heading not required.)

Instructions regarding War Diaries and Intelligence Summaries are contained in F. S. Regs., Part II. and the Staff Manual respectively. Title pages will be prepared in manuscript.

Place	Date	Hour	Summary of Events and Information	Remarks and references to Appendices
In the Field.	AUGUST. 29th.		Bn. in Divisional Reserve. The G.O.C. 29th. Division visited the Camp during the morning. Company Training was carried out.	
	30th.		Bn. in Divisional Reserve. "D" Company relieved "A" Coy in the STRAZEELE defences.	
	31st.		Bn. in Divisional Reserve. Company Training was carried out.	

J R French Major
for Lieut. Colonel.
Commanding 2nd. Battalion Leinster Regiment.

OPERATION ORDER NO 25
by
Lieut Col E.W Weldon, Comdg 2nd Devonshire Regt   25 Aug 1918

COPY NO 9

INFORM 1. The Batt. will relieve the 1st Border Regt tonight in the front line

2. Companies will move from the present position in the following order D.C.B.A. & 6th. The leading Coy will move at 8 pm. Distance of 100 yds to be maintained between platoons. Route to be followed —
W.21.d, SC.40, STRAZEELE, ERIN COTTAGE

INTENTION 3. D Coy Lewisters will relieve D Coy Borders   (LEFT FRONT)
                    C   H   (RIGHT FRONT)
                    B   B   (LEFT SUPPORT)
                    A   C   (RIGHT SUPPORT)

4. Guides will meet Coys at Batln H.Q. (X.27.d.2.8.) as under
A & B Coy Leinsters - 1 p. platoon 1 per Coy H.Q. C Coy Leinsters - 1 per platoon 1 of these men will also guide Coy H.Q.

DETAILS 5. One limber per Coy will report at Coy H.Q. at 7 pm. These will carry Lewis Guns and S.A.A. ammn. and will move under Coy arrangements

6. On arrival in the line limbers will return to Transport

7. The following stores will be at the Battn. dump (ANDERSONS) FARM or as far along R tracks in advance of Battn H.Qrs as possible and thence be carried up by Coys to their lines.
One day RATIONS. WATER 15 tins per front line Coy, 10 tins per support Coy.
SHOVELS 90 per front line Coy.

(a) Each man will carry two bandoliers which will be issued before the Battalion moves from present positions

6. All defence schemes, maps & intelligence notes, S.A.A. and Verey Pistols will be taken over and list of same forwarded to Battn. H.Q. by 6 pm 25 inst.

7. Gaps between posts should be covered by Lewis Guns

8. Liaison between platoons, Coys and Battns will be established by interlocking posts between units on right and left flanks in front and support lines to be established and the liaison forwarded to Battn. H.Qrs as soon as possible.

9. A Sketch map showing tactical position of all posts should be forwarded to Battn H.Qrs by 6am 26 inst. This must be accurate.

10. R.A.P. to be at Battn. H.Qrs.

11. Demands for R.E. Stores, S.A.A. Verey lights, S.O.S. Signals etc (if required) to be made as soon as possible.

12. Completion of relief to be notified to these H.Qrs by code word HELL

A.D. Keye
Adjt. 2nd Leinster Regt.

Issued at 5.15 pm
Copies 1. A
        2. B
        3. C
        4. D
        5. HQ
        6. 6th
        7. Bde
        8. Brigade
        9. Coy Diary
        10. File

OPERATION ORDERS No 26
Lt Col X W Weldon Comdg 2nd Leinster Regt.   Aug 23/18

STRAZEELE

1. The Battn will be relieved in the Left Sector on the night 23/24
Aug by the 2nd Hants Regt and will take over Reserve positions held
by that Battn.

2. Order of Relief.
    Y Coy Hants will relieve 2 platoons C Coy (Lewis ers) in Outpost Line
    W   2 platoons C   }   in front line RIGHT
    X   D   }   in front line LEFT
    Z   D Coy   in Support line
                                   2 platoons B Coy }   Reserve line
                                    A Coy   }

    On completion of above
    A Coy Leinsters will take over Old Front Line RIGHT from Y Coy 2nd Hants
    B   LEFT   X
    C   STRAZEELE defences   Z
    D   in E.6.a.   W
    Battn H.Q. will be at POTAM HOUSE W.29.d.13.

3. Advance Parties 1 Officer per Coy and 1 OR per platoon will proceed to
reconnoitre new positions and take over stores &c. Advance party of
A + B Coys will return to their Coys and act as Guides after 1st Relief.

4. Guides. 1 Guide per platoon and 1 for Coy HQrs. will report at Battn
H.Q. at 9.p.m. Guides for A+B Coy to new positions will not be
necessary. Guides for C + D Coys will be at present Battn H.Qrs in
readiness to take Coys to new positions.

5. Stores. All turn to stores will be handed over to the incoming unit also
Iron Rations & SAA (Very stores lists not necessary)

6. Transport. None is wanted for A+B Coys 2 limbers each per C + D Coys
will be at Ration Dump at 9 pm. Limbers and Cookers leave for
Baths HQrs at 9.30 pm. Coy Mess Cart.

7. Blankets will be handed over in a scrupulously clean condition
and receipts obtained.

8. Completion of relief to be reported by code message "FIRST"
occupation of new positions reported by code message "SECOND"

                                                Whitehead Capt.
                                                Adjt 2 Leinster Regt.

COPY NO 1

OPERATION ORDER NO 27.
Capt V.J. Farrell MC. Comdg 2nd Leinster Regt.

Reference Map STRAZEELE   Aug 26th 1918

I The Battn. will be relieved in Brigade Support on the 26th Aug and will take over Z line in reserve to 87th Inf Brigade under whose orders they will come on completion.

II Order of relief.
    "A" Coy 1st K.O.S.Bs will relieve A Coy Leinsters in old British front line LEFT
    "B"   B   RIGHT
    "D"   C   in STRAZEELE defences
    "C"   D   MONT MERRIS defences

On completion Companies will take over Z line in the following order from RIGHT to LEFT. A.B.D.C. Battn H.Qrs will move to BRICK WORKS. W.22.d.9.8.

III Advance parties of 1 Officer per Coy and 1 OR per platoon will take over from 2n S.W.Bs at 4 pm.

IV Guides for 1st K.O.S.Bs will be provided as per arrangements between Company Commanders. Guides for Z line will not be required, the advance party will meet Coys at points to be selected by Coy Comders with details of new positions.

V Transport Lewis Gun limbers will meet A & B Coys at Ration Dump F.1.b.9.6 at 9.30 pm. for Lewis Guns and Petrol Tins. No transport required for C & D Coys. 1 limber and Maltese Cart at Battn H.Q. 8.30 pm.

VI Rations will be delivered to new locations

VII Trench Stores Ammunition etc will be handed over, lists to be at O Room by 10am 27th inst also certificate of cleanliness of trenches handed over.

VIII Completion of relief will be reported by Code Message "PREMIER" arrival in new locations by code word "SECUNDUS"

A.S. Whitehead
Capt.
Adjt. 2n Leinster Regt.

OPERATION ORDERS No.29.   COPY.....2

Reference SHEET 27.   30th. August.1918.

1. An inter Company relief will take place tonight 30th. August, "D" Company relieving "A" Company in STRAZEELE Defences and coming under orders of G.O.C. 86th. Infantry Brigade.

2. "D" Company will parade at 5 p.m. less nucleus (Minimum 11) who will remain in Camp.

3. On completion "A" Company will join Battalion in Camp V.23.a.1.9.

4. An advance party of 1 Officer & 1 O.R. per platoon will proceed at 2 p.m. to take over and allot positions.

5. Trench Stores will be handed over by "A" Company and receipt obtained.

6. TRANSPORT. 1 Limber will report at Camp at 4.30 p.m. for Lewis Guns & Dixies and accompany "D" Company - returning with "A" Companys Guns and Dixies.

7. Arrival in Camp of "A" Company to be reported to Adjutant.

                                    Sd. A.H. Whitehead.   Captain,
                        Adjutant 2nd. Battn. Leinster Regiment.

DISTRIBUTION.
COPY No. 1. C.O.
        2. Adjutant.
        3. O.C. "A" Coy.
        4. O.C. "D" Coy.
        5. Quartermaster.
        6. R.T.O.
        7. H.Q. 88th. Inf. Brigade.
        8. H.Q. 86th. "   "
        9. File.

CONFIDENTIAL

WAR DIARY

of

2nd Battalion, The Leinster Regiment

From 1st September To 30th September, 1918.

(VOLUME NO 6).

Army Form 2118.

WAR DIARY
or
INTELLIGENCE SUMMARY. 2nd LEINSTER REGT.

(Erase heading not required.)

Instructions regarding War Diaries and Intelligence Summaries are contained in F. S. Regs., Part II. and the Staff Manual respectively. Title pages will be prepared in manuscript.

ORDERLY ROOM
No. 4786
5 OCT 1918
2nd Bn. LEINSTER REGT

Place	Date	Hour	Summary of Events and Information	Remarks and references to Appendices
In the Field.	SEPTEMBER. 1st.		The Battalion less "D" Coy. embussed at LA KREULE at 7.15 a.m. and debussed 1 kilo. W. of BAILLEUL. Route:- CAESTRE - METRE - METEREN. Battalion then marched to RAVELSBURG (28 S.W. S.15.b.d.16.a.c.) and bivouacked there. "D" Coy. rejoined in the afternoon. Capt.J.A.J.Farrell.D.S.O. was attached to 88th. Bde. H.Q. as Liason Officer. The Battalion went into Bde. Reserve. The following officers went in:- R.Qrs., Lt.Col.H.W.Weldon - Capt. A.H.Whitehead.M.C.,2/Lt.S.O'C.Mullins. Lieut. Newson. U.S.R., - Capt. J.MacSheehan.M.C. (C.R.). "A" Coy:- Lieut.Sander,2/Lieut.Delaney,2/Lieut.Davis,Lieut.Smythe. "B" Coy:- Lieut.Keating,Lieut. MacNamara,2/Lt.Wylde,2/Lieut.Pearson. "C" Coy:- Capt.V.F.Farrell.M.C.,2/Lt.Woods.M.C., 2/Lt.Holden,2/Lieut.Hickey. "D" Coy:- Capt.G.E.Farrell,2/Lieut.Tricks,2/Lieut.Johnston,2/Lieut.Snookes.	
	2nd.		Battalion in Brigade Reserve. - Quiet day.	
	3rd.		Battalion moved to PENGUIN Camp (28 S.W./S.29) and had dinner there. At 8 p.m. the Battn. proceeded to 28S.W./T.16.& 17 the assembly position for the attack on HILL 63 arranged for tomorrow, the Germans having concluded their retreat. Lieut.Morris rejoined from leave.	
	4th.		The Battn. went over at 8 a.m. At 7 a.m. the enemy opened destructive artillery fire on our positions and kept it up till 7.45 a.m. under cover of a heavy ground barrage "A" & "D" Coys advanced in two waves. "B" Company were detailed to follow as moppers up. "C" Company were in Reserve. Our barrage was splendid. - The enemy reply tho' vigourous was uneven. About 1000 yards on, to the W of the road running approximately N/S thro' T.17 central, a strong band of wire was found to have been put out by the enemy. His M.G's from the crest of the hill played on to it, and hung our advance up for a few minutes. Our Troops however forced their way thro' with determination and continued the advance on Hill 63. As soon as we had forced the wire, most of the enemy began to retire hastily, but small M.G. posts continued firing. Some of these were accounted for by the first waves and "B" Company, while the remainder were killed or captured by "C" Company which had swung in from the left. The first waves swept some 500 yards beyond the objective and held on there for about 2 hours. Owing to our flanks not getting on so well, they were eventually withdrawn to the objective line which ran:- 28 S.W./T.12.d.0.8.- d.4.o.- U.13.a.oo.75.- The Cellars - LaRossignol. Captures. 74 prisoners, 2 light T.M's, 9 M.G's,1 anti tank gun and a messenger dog. Prisoners	

A6945. Wt. W14422/M160 350,000 12/16 D. D. & L. Forms/C./2118/14.

Army Form 2118.

WAR DIARY
or
INTELLIGENCE SUMMARY.
(Erase heading not required.)

Place	Date	Hour	Summary of Events and Information	Remarks and references to Appendices
In the Field.	4th.		belonged to 156th. I.R. of the 11th. Res. Div. and stated that we had captured their main line of resistance. About 1.30 p.m. it was reported that the enemy were creeping up on the left. The artillery laid down a light 18 pdr. barrage and this action appeared to be effective. From 10 a.m. onwards the enemy harassed the front area with field guns His snipers and machine gunners were active on our front line, especially so on the parts destroyed by shell fire. This activity was kept up during the whole day, but slackened off at night. Our casualties the heavy, were light in comparison to the importance of the advance. 2/Lieut. V.A. Davis ("A" COY) was killed by a sniper at 11 a.m. Capt. G.E.Farrell, Lt.Sander, Lt. Smythe, 2/Lt.Tricks and Delamay were wounded. Casualties amongst Other Ranks:- Killed 26, Wounded 118, Missing 16. Battalion Headquarters moved from G.H.Q. Line at Zero plus 15 and proceeded to T.18.a.2.1. 2 Companies of the 4th. Worcestershire Regt. were attached to the Battalion during the afternoon - one as Counter Attack Company, the other to fill the gap between us and the 2nd. Hampshire Regt. who had advanced simultaneously with us. The Final Battalion frontage was approximately 1500 yards. On our right, the R.D.F. captured PLOEGSTEERT with 100 prisoners. Small parties of Germans continued to try to creep round on our right, but were dealt with by the 2nd. Hants. The 4th. Worcester Regt supplied a carrying party on the night for rations, water and ammunition. Our advance was 3000 yards over country studded with ditches, corpses and old defences. The Hill is steep and bristles with defensive positions. The final rush of our men up the slopes excited the admiration of all who saw it. EN PASSANT, 2 Battalions in 1916 achieved what 3 Divisions found a hard task in 1914.	
	5th.		Battalion in Front Line. The enemy was reported to be massing against the Brigade on our left. The Counter Attack Company of the 4th. Worcestershire Regt was therefore held at its disposal. No attack took place. In the evening the Battalion was relieved by the 24th. R.Welsh Fusiliers and the 12th. Norfolk Regt (31st. Division). Two Companies of the Welsh Fusiliers took over the Brigade Front line and 2 companies of the Norfolks relieved the Support companies On relief, B.H.Q., "A" "C" & "D" Coys. proceeded to COMET CAMP, while "B" Coy. marched to Camp at X.18 between BAILLEUL and METEREN.	
	6th.		The Battalion less "B" Coy marched to Camp at X.16. The day was devoted to resting.	

Army Form 2118.

WAR DIARY
or
INTELLIGENCE SUMMARY.
(Erase heading not required.)

Instructions regarding War Diaries and Intelligence Summaries are contained in F.S. Regs., Part II. and the Staff Manual respectively. Title pages will be prepared in manuscript.

Place	Date	Hour	Summary of Events and Information	Remarks and references to Appendices
In the Field.	7th.		The C.O. attended a Divisional Conference after which he lectured the Officers on some of the lessons of the attack. The following messages were published in Battalion Orders;-	
			(a) From General Sir. H. PLUMER, Commanding II Army to Lt.General Sir B. de Lisle, Commanding XVth. Corps.- "Please accept yourself and convey to 20th. Division my heartiest congratulations on their successful operation yesterday. The capture of Hill 63 was of the utmost importance and was brilliantly carried out as was also the capture of PLOEGSTREET."	
			(b) From Lt.General. Sir B. de Lisle, Commanding XVth. Corps to Major.General Cavley, commanding 20th. Division.- "I send you the Army Commanders message and wish you to inform, Brigades and all Units concerned how highly I appreciate their gallant action yesterday.	
			(c) The C.O. wishes to express his admiration to the Officers for their leadership and to the N.C.O.s and men for the splendid manner in which they effected the capture of Hill 63. A draft of 45 Other Ranks arrived.	
	8th.		The Battalion attended R.C. Divine Service in Camp at 10 a.m. The G.O.C. 88th. Brigade spoke to the Officers of the Battalion expressing his appreciation of the recent operation. Major.General CAVLEY visited the Camp during the morning.	
	9th.		Company Training.- Capt.J.A.J. Farrell D.S.O. left to become 2nd. in Command of the 7th. London Regiment, 58th. Division.	
	10th.		Company Training. 2/Lieut. TOOLAN rejoined from 36th. Division.	
	11th.		The Battalion struck camp and marched to billets in the School House and houses on the RUE L'ORPHELINAT, HAZEBROUCK.	
	12th.		The Battalion was inspected in "Battle Order" by the G.O.- 2/Lieut. O'Brien and Lieut. Cade joined from the Base.- 2/Lieut. O'Brien took over the duties of Signalling Officer temporarily	
	13th.		Company Training. 2/Lieut. Beavan joined from the base. The 88th. F.A. gave a Concert in the Theatre for the 2nd. Leinster Regiment.	
	14th.		Company Training.	
	15th.		R.C's.Church in MORBECQUE ROAD at 10 a.m.	

Army Form 2118.

WAR DIARY
or
INTELLIGENCE SUMMARY.
(Erase heading not required.)

Instructions regarding War Diaries and Intelligence Summaries are contained in F.S. Regs., Part II. and the Staff Manual respectively. Title pages will be prepared in manuscript.

Place	Date	Hour	Summary of Events and Information	Remarks and references to Appendices
In the Field.	15th.		Presbyterians and Non-Conformists.- Send Billet IDCom.- C of Es.- Theatre at 11 a.m.	
	16th.		Company Training. The Battalion practised an attack and its exploitation scheme in the afternoon.	
	17th.		Battalion paraded for Baths in V.17. In the afternoon a pow wow was held, attended by Officers and N.C.Os.- Brigadier General Freyberg V.C.,D.S.O. address it.	
	18th.		Company Training.	
	19th.		Company Training.- A Battalion Concert was held in the theatre in the evening. A draft of 38 Other Ranks arrived from the base.	
	20th.		Company Training. A series of boxing was held in the evening between the Battalion and the 2nd. Hants.- The Battalion was successful in all save 1 bout.	
	21st.		Battalion entrained at HONDEGHEM at 9.30 p.m. and came on in two trains to ST. JAN TER BIEZEN (Sheet 28) going into Camp at Roads Camp (F.25.c.)	
	22nd.		The G.O.C. II Corps (under whose orders the 29th. Div. now are) met the C.O's., Adjts., Company Commanders, and I.O's of the Brigade at the 2nd. Worcester H.Q. Mess. Reconnoitring parties afterwards went up E of YPRES.	
	23rd.		Battalion in Roads Camp.	
	24th.		Battalion entrained for YPRES and detrained at GOLD FISH CHATEAU (28/H.11.a.c.) The Battalion relieved the 5.R.B's and a Company of the 1st. Lancs. Fusiliers in Support in the ZILLEBEKE Sector. Companies were disposed as under:-	
			"B" & "C" Companies in BOBSTAY CASTLE. defences (H.12.a.b.)	
			"A" in the ECOLE (1c/c)	
			"D" in MOATE TRENCH (I.14.b.)	
			B.H.Q. in the RAMPARTS.	
			The following officers went in:- BnH.Q.- Lt.Colonel.H.W.Weldon, Capt. A.H.Whitehead.M.C., Capt.MacSheehan M.B.(C.F.) Lieut.Owen-Morris (R.A.M.C.), 2/Lt.McMahon, 2/Lt.S.O'C.Mullins	

A6945 Wt.W1422/M1160 350,000 12/16 D.D.&L. Forms/C/2118/14.

WAR DIARY
or
INTELLIGENCE SUMMARY
(Erase heading not required.)

Army Form 2118.

Place	Date	Hour	Summary of Events and Information	Remarks and references to Appendices
	24th.		"A" Coy.- Capt.Whittington,Lt.Goode,2/Lt.Shelly,2/Lt.Toolen.	
			"B" Coy.- Capt.Keating,Capt.Mathias,Lt.MacDonald,2/Lt.Morrison.	
			"C" Coy.- Capt.V.J.Farrell M.C., Lt.Hitchcock M.C., 2/Lt.Fitz-Simon,2/Lt.Miller.	
			"D" Coy.- Capt.Moran,2/Lt.Hutcninson,2/Lt.Johnston,2/Lt.O'Brien,2/Lt.Midgeley.	
	25th.		Battalion in Support. - Quiet Day. The following N.C.Os. & O'Rs. were awarded the M.M. for gallantry during the Hill 63 operations.	
			4077 Sgt. Costello, 7178 Sgt. P.McCray, 411 L/Sergt.J.O'Niell,5304 Cpl.A.Bricknell, 18355 Cpl.M.Murphy, 4277 Cpl. C.J.Horan, 5372 Pte.W.Beames,511 Pte.L.Butler 695 Pte.B.Cole, 18125 Pte.T.Halligen,5509 Pte.R.Denman, 7094 Pte. P.McAuliffe, 3653 Pte.M.O'Brien, 5077 Pte. R.Reddy.	
	26th.		The Battalion was relieved in Brigade Support in the evening by the 87th. Brigade and moved to the YPRES defences. "D" Coy. remained in MOATE TRENCH, "A" Coy. were disposed of in MOAT TRENCH from I.18.d.8.5. to MENIN Road.; "B" & "C" in Infantry Barracks. B.H.Q. in RAMPARTS, YPRES.	
	27th.		The Battalion moved to assembly position (see attached map and O.O.) at dusk.	
	28th.		The Belgian Army opened a bombardment at 2:30 a.m. At 5.30 a.m. in conjunction with the Belgians, the 2nd. Corps attacked the Germans from DIXMUDE to S.E. of YPRES. The 20th. Division per 88th. and 87th. Brigades and captured all objectives. The 88th. Bde followed over in Reserveand was pushed thro' to exploit success. The 2nd. Leinster Regiment left the assembly position at 6 plus 45 and marched down the MENIN ROAD, pipers playing and flag flying to HOOGE. Hence the Battalion advanced on diamond formation to GHELUVELT, where it concentrated. The Battalion being in Reserve, the Worcesters and Hants pushed on. "B" and "C" Coys were pushed on towards GHELUVELT Wood in the afternoon and advanced as far as 100 yards E of Cross Roads in J.3.c. At night "B" and "C" attempted to reach the line J.3.1.a.Central "B" got there, but "C" were unable to owing to strong opposition. "B" was accordingly withdrawn to conform with C's line.	

Army Form 2118.

WAR DIARY
or
INTELLIGENCE SUMMARY.

(Erase heading not required.)

Place	Date	Hour	Summary of Events and Information	Remarks and references to Appendices
In the Field.	29th.		Battalion received orders to concentrate in J.30.c. The Battalion remained in Shell holes for the night, during torrential rain.	
	30th.		It having been reported that GHELUVE had fallen, the Battalion resumed the advance, passing thro' the Worcesters. "D" advanced on the left of the MENIN ROAD to the line K.3.a.c.7.- b.c.c. "A" and "C" were sent in on the right, but could make no progress owing to heavy opposition. "B" Company relieved "D" Coy at night. The 2nd. Hants "A" Coy moved to K.33.c. "C" Company remained where it was, in advance of the Hampshire line. Heavy rain fell. The following Officers were wounded during the 3 days operations: Capt. Mathias, 2/Lt. Toolen, 2/Lt. Mts-Simon, 2/Lt.Miller went down sick.	

4.10.1918.

M Whitehead
Capt ɑ/a/11
Lieut.Colonel,
Commanding 2nd. Battalion Leinster Regiment.

CONFIDENTIAL

WAR DIARY

of

2nd Battalion The Leinster Regiment

From 1st October To 31st October, 1918.

(VOLUME NO.7).

WAR DIARY
or
INTELLIGENCE SUMMARY

Army Form C. 2118.

October 1918.

Place	Date	Hour	Summary of Events and Information	Remarks and references to Appendices
Chat 28 GHELUVE	1st		Bn. in front line. Our posts were heavily shelled and machine gunned. Owing to the strength of the enemy and the weakened condition of the men, it was decided to discontinue the advance. In the evg. B coy. was relieved in the front line by the 2nd Hampshire Regt. and the Bn. less D coy. bivouacked in 28 J 36 b and 30 d, forming the Bde. reserve. D coy. remained in K 33 as support to the front Bn.	M
	2nd		D coy. was relieved in support in the evening and rejoined Bn. in J 36 b. Casualties to the Bn. since 28th ult. as follows: Killed – 19. Wounded – 129. Missing – 10.	M
BRANDHOEK Area	3rd		The 29th Divn. was relieved in the front area. The Bn. left J 36 at 1500 hours and marched to BIRR CROSS ROADS, entraining there at 1900 hours for TAVISTOCK CAMP (28 H 1).	M
	4th		Bn. in Rest. The following message of appreciation from Lt.-Gen. Sir Claud Jacob K.C.B. cmdg. II Army Corps was published in Bn. orders. To G.O.C. 29th Divn.	M

WAR DIARY
or
~~INTELLIGENCE SUMMARY~~

Army Form C.2118.

Place	Date	Hour	Summary of Events and Information	Remarks and references to Appendices
BRANDHOEK			"The Division you have the honour to command has won glory and distinction wherever it has served during this war. The operations which it has undertaken since 28th September 1918 have added still more to the fame of the 29th Divn. The Division was specially selected for these operations and it has carried them out without a hitch from first to last. When it is remembered that in 1917 it took over 3 months to gain the PASSCHENDAELE - BROODSEINDE Ridge and how costly those operations were, it redounds greatly to the credit of the 29th Division that not only did they capture the ridge but also the ground far beyond in less than 24 hours. It was a great achievement and I offer you and all ranks my heartiest congratulations and thanks for all you have done. The capture of GHELUVELT and GHELUWE is a most important event as so much depended on getting well down over and beyond the ridge. You have had hard fighting at GHELUWE and the weather conditions were bad, but in spite of all that, you have added still more glory to the splendid name the 29th Division has always borne since the Division was first formed.	JH JH JH

WAR DIARY
or
INTELLIGENCE SUMMARY.
(Erase heading not required.)

Army Form C. 2118.

Place	Date	Hour	Summary of Events and Information	Remarks and references to Appendices
			There is still hard fighting before us, but with such troops as yours, no Commander need have any anxiety as to the results of any operations you are called upon to undertake. My heartiest congratulations to you, your Brigadiers Staffs and all ranks." (Sgd) C.W. Jacob. Lt Gen. Comg. II Army Corps.	
YPRES	5/9/18		Bn. in rest. In the afternoon the Bn. moved up to YPRES, companies being disposed in the RAMPARTS and surrounding area. The following officers came up with the Bn.	
			B.H.Q. – Lt.Col. WELDON. Capt. V. FARRELL M.C. Lt. NIE (ADJT.) 2/Lt. MACNAMARA. 2/Lt. S. O/C. MULLINS. Capt. Rev. J.J. MacSHEEHAN. C.F. M.C. Lt. OWEN-MORRIS. R.A.M.C.	
			A Coy. – Capt. R.H. SANDER. Lt. COADE. 2/Lt. BARKER M.C. 2/Lt. APPLEYARD.	
			B Coy. – 2/Lt. WYLDE. Lt. MOORE. Lt. J.de C. MacDONALD. 2/Lt. PEARSON.	
			C Coy. – Capt. WHITTINGTON. Capt. LEWIS. 2/Lt. HICKEY. O'BRIEN. Lt. STEYNES.	
			D Coy. – Capt. MORAN. 2/Lt. DALTON. O'SULLIVAN SMITH.	
			The following decorations were announced:	
			D.S.O. – Capt. V.T. FARRELL M.C.	
			M.C. – 2/Lt. W. McCARTHY (att 88 T.M.B)	
			D.C.M. – 3775 C.S.M. T. FENNELL. 6945 Pte. M. BYRNE Emm (ad bar.) Pte. BARRY. Pte. O'GRADY.	

Army Form C.118.

WAR DIARY
or
INTELLIGENCE SUMMARY.

(Erase heading not required.)

Place	Date	Hour	Summary of Events and Information	Remarks and references to Appendices
YPRES	Feb 1918 6.		Bn. in Reserve at YPRES.	R.
WESTHOEK	7.		88th Bde. went into Support. Bn. relieved the 1st BORDER REGT. in support in camp at WESTHOEK.	M.S.
"	8.		Bde. in Support. Company Training. G.O.C. 29th Division visited the Bn. and had tea at Hd. Quarters.	R.
LEDEGHEM	9.		Bn. relieved the 2nd Royal Fusiliers in the front line LEDEGHEM sector. A and B took over the front line, C came into Support and D into Reserve. B.H.Q. 28K.12a5,9. 300 additional yards of front were taken over by 2 platoons of D coy from 9th Divn.	R.W.
	10.		Bn. in front line. Quiet day. Two daylight patrols under N.C.O's. went out to obtain an identification, unsuccessfully. Our second patrol lost 1 o.r. killed and 1 o.r. wounded. In the evening the 4th WORCESTERs relieved the Bn. of its frontage SOUTH of the HEULEBEEK. A Coy on relief took over the 9th Divn. Frontage.	R.

WAR DIARY
or
INTELLIGENCE SUMMARY.
(Erase heading not required.)

Army Form C. 2118.

Place	Date	Hour	Summary of Events and Information	Remarks and references to Appendices
LEDEGHEM	Oct 1918		up to 28L2a97, B coy advanced their right post 150 yards, meeting no opposition	
	11.		Bn. in front line. Quiet day. In the evg. 86th Bde. was relieved and moved into Reserve. The 1st S.W.B. relieved the Bn. which moved to camp at NORDENHOEK (BECELAERE area) the route being picketed by the 2nd Hants.	M/
BECELAERE	12.		Bn. in Reserve. Heavy rain fell all day.	M/
	13.		Bn. in Reserve. In the evg. the Bn. moved up into their assembly position encountering some heavy shelling. Map A shows assembly area. B coy was placed in position North of the KEULEBEEK, the remainder of the Bn. being South of this stream.	M/
LEDEGHEM	14.		At 0535 hours the 2nd Corps attacked in conjunction with Franco-Belgian armies. The 29th Divn. attacked for 86th and 88th Bdes. in the LEDEGHEM sector. A.B. and C. coys. of the Bn. advanced in the first wave and penetrated to a depth of 4,100 yards. A dense fog lay over the ground and was thickened by the intense barrage laid	M/

WAR DIARY
or
INTELLIGENCE SUMMARY.
(Erase heading not required.)

Army Form C.118.

Place	Date	Hour	Summary of Events and Information	Remarks and references to Appendices
Sh 1 29			down. Consequently several gaps were left in the line of attack and many m/guns were passed over which continued in action for some time after they had been officially captured. A German Field Battery unconscious of having been passed continued firing until charged by D coy. (Company in Reserve) Close on time we reached our objective, the road running from L.12 central - BERT FORK - Fm TILLEUL. Altho' the enemy was expecting an attack and had made preparations against it, no very great resistance was met with, the usual intense machine-gunning of the enemy being rendered harder to stop by the fog. Defence is greatly assisted here by the nature of the country, studded as it is with woods, farms and villages. Our captures were by 1- 14 officers and 249 o.r.s. 60 m.g.'s (of which B coy. captured 48.) and 11 guns of various calibres chiefly field guns. Our casualties amounted to 2 officers and 90 o.r.s killed. 5 officers and 70 o.r.s wounded, and 5 o.r. missing. Officer casualties were Lt. Moore (B) and Lt. J. de Courcy MacDonald (B) killed; Capt. R.H. Sanders (A) 2/Lt. Barker m.c.(A) Lt. Coade (A) 2/Lt. H. Wylde (B) and Capt. Van Cutsem (Batt. at.) wounded. At 1100 hours the 2nd Hants passed thro' the 4th Worcesters coming into support.	1 /h /h /h /h

WAR DIARY
or
INTELLIGENCE SUMMARY.

Army Form 2118.

Place	Date	Hour	Summary of Events and Information	Remarks and references to Appendices
Sherton	Oct. 1918		The Bn. was withdrawn and reorganised into 3 companies — A under Capt. Lewis, B and C under Capt. Whittington and D under Capt. Moran. In the evening the Bn. billeted in the OVERHEULE area.	M
	15.		The Bn. moved from OVERHEULE at 1000 hours. As the 87" Bde. had gained 4000 yards in the morning, the Bn. moved up into the SAULNER area, billeting there for the night.	M
	16.		The 88 Bde. relieved the 87" Bde. in the front area. The Bn. went into Reserve and moved into the HEULE area, billeting 10.29C.11 E. and 612. D.H.Q. at 29 G. 12 a 4.3.	M
	17.		Bn. in Bde. Reserve. A Coy was sent to CUERNE to evacuate the civilian population.	M
	18.		Bn. in Bde. Reserve. Lt. W. Cooper Condr. M.M's.C. awarded the following D.S.O.	(M)

WAR DIARY
INTELLIGENCE SUMMARY.
(Erase heading not required.)

Army Form C.2118.

Place	Date	Hour	Summary of Events and Information	Remarks and references to Appendices
Shulega	6/6/18		For gallantry and devotion to duty in the Field for the 28th Sept. operations:— 16038 Pte. W. BONNIFACE (B), 2288 Pte. J. BURKE, 5229, Pte. J.P. FLOOD, 2982 Cpl. R. McGUCKIN, 10876 Pte. G. MOLLEY, 15237 Pte. T. HOWE, 18176 Pte. P. LALLY, 18125 Pte. T. HALLIGAN, 16779 Pte. F.J. SENIOR. D.C.M.	M
	19.		Bn. in Bde. Reserve. Capt. A.H. WHITEHEAD M.C. rejoined from hospital and resumed duties of Adjt. Bn. received orders to concentrate in H14 and 20 in preparation for an attack on 20th inst. Bn. was in position by 22.00 hours. Shortly before, 2 coys of the 2nd Hants effected a crossing of the L/S between COURTRAI and HARLEBEKE and proceeded to mop up our assembly position. Bn. crossed the L/S by pontoon bridge and proceeded to take up position the line of the railway in 29.H.22.c-28.a. A coy was unable to take up its position till 04.00 hours on 20th owing to the enemy's occupation of it.	M
	20.		Bn. attacked in conjunction with the 4th WORCESTERS at 06.00 hours under a light barrage. The villages of STACEGHEM and STEENBRUGGE was captured. Hostile resistance	

WAR DIARY or INTELLIGENCE SUMMARY

Army Form C. 2118

Place	Date	Hour	Summary of Events and Information	Remarks and references to Appendices
Shul-29 ?mons	19/9/18		Weak at first gradually stiffened and east of STACEGHEM the advance was carried out under very heavy machine gun fire — the road running from 29.I.27.a.70 to I.32.c.98. This constitutes the objective line — the was reached and consolidated by 0920 hours. An advance of 5000 yards. 40 prisoners were captured and 6 m.guns and 1 field gun. On consolidation, orders at little HANTS who passed thro' at 1030 hours. The remainder was attached to C company was ADC from left to right. B coy in part went further on with the 2nd and 3 officers (Major REDWAY, Lt. SMITH and 2/Lt. FLANNERY)	M
			Casualties:- 6 o.r. killed, 3 officers (Major REDWAY, Lt. SMITH and 2/Lt. FLANNERY) and 70 o.r. wounded. B.H.Q. at STEENBRUGGE. In the afternoon the 88th Bde. was relieved by the 76 Bde. and the Bn. was withdrawn to billets in the STACEGHEM area. B.H.Q. at H.28.d.6.6.	
	21.		Bn. in Reserve.	M
	22.		Bn. in Reserve.	M
	23.		Bn. in Reserve. G.O.C. 29 Divn. visited the Bn. in the morning. MARSHAL	M

WAR DIARY
or
INTELLIGENCE SUMMARY.

(Erase heading not required.)

Army Form C. 2118.

Place	Date	Hour	Summary of Events and Information	Remarks and references to Appendices
Shol	Oct 1918 23		Foch sent a message from II Army H.Q. congratulating the 29th Division on its gallant work. The 29th Divn. was relieved by the 41st Divn.	Appx
	24.		Bn. in Rest. Coy. Training.	
	25.		Bn. in Rest. Coy. Training.	Appx
	26.		Bn. moved by route march to RISQUONS-TOUT (2 km. N. of TURCOING) at 0600 hours, arriving at 1300 hours. The Bn. was inspected en route by Maj. Gen. CAYLEY. The Bn. billeted in the hospital for the night.	Appx
	27.		Bn. marched to CROIX at 0900 hours. Route - TURCOING - ROUBAIX - CROIX, where the Bn. was billeted. Lt. Gen. Sir H. de B. de LISLE, C. of S. XV Corps took the salute at CROIX. The Bn. was inspected on the march in the Square at ROUBAIX by G.O.C. 88th Bde. 29th Divn. & once more under XV Corps orders.	Appx

Army Form 2118.

WAR DIARY
or
INTELLIGENCE SUMMARY.
(Erase heading not required.)

Place	Date	Hour	Summary of Events and Information	Remarks and references to Appendices
Sturz.	Oct 1918			
	28.		Bn. in Rest billets.	M.
	29.		Bn. Parade and Company Training.	M.
	30.		Bn. took part in the rehearsal for the 88- Bde. Ceremonial Parade arranged for Nov 1st Bn. Sm. FREYBERG VC. DSO. communicated a message of appreciation of the gallant work performed by the Division since 28th Sept from Gen Sir H. PLUMER Cmdg. II Army. A draft of 1 officer (Lt. WARBURTON) and 64 O.R. arrived in the evg.	M.
	31.		Bn. Parade and Company Training. In the month under review, the Bn. has advanced nearly mast advances amounting to nearly 10,000 yards captures 5 villages and taken 306 prisoners, 66 machine guns and 12 field guns.	M.

J. Walker Lt. Colonel
Commanding 2nd Bn. the Lincoln Regiment

OPERATION ORDER No 35
BY
Lt Col H.W. Weldon Comdg 2nd Lancaster Regt.

Ref Sheet 28. 40,000
Oct 6th 1918

1. The Battn will move to the WEST HOEK area by march route tomorrow the 7th inst and will relieve the 1st Border Regt.
   Transport lines and Q.M. Stores will not move.

2. Advance Party (one N.C.O. per Coy and one N.C.O. from H.Q. will parade under 2nd Lieut Mellins at 7.45 am at the MENIN GATE, and will report to Staff Capt. at 87th Bde H.Q. at I.8.a.0.3 at 9 am.

3. Rations for consumption on the 8th inst will be delivered by the train to present Transport Lines.

4. Copies of receipts for French Shelters taken over will be handed to the Adjutant by 3 pm.

5. Lewis Gun limbers will report to Coys at 8.30 am. The Mess Cart and Maltese Cart will report at Battn H.Q. at the same time. Blankets rolled in bundles of ten and Officers kits to be stacked by Companies by 8 am. Baggage waggons provided by Brigade will carry blankets and kits, Cookers will move with the Battn. Dinners will be cooked on the march.

6. The Battn HQ will parade at 9.50 am in the following order: A.B.C.D. DRESS. Battle Order Great Coats rolled in waterproof sheets. The Battn will be formed up on the main YPRES road with the head of the column at the MENIN GATE. Intervals of 25 yards between Coys. Lewis Gun Limbers to follow respective Coys.

7. Particular care will be taken that all billets are handed over in a clean and sanitary condition. Certificates to the effect will be handed to the Adjutant at 9.45 am.

Issued at 10.30 pm.

A Dhy. Lieut
Adjt 2 Lancaster Regt.

OPERATION ORDER No 36

Lt Col H.W Weldon Comdg 2 Leinster Regt

Ref Sheet 28 NE. 1/20.000

Oct 8th 1918

1. The Bath will relieve the 2nd Royal Fusiliers in the line on the night of 10 October as follows :- A Coy right front B Coy left front "C" Coy Support "D" Coy reserve. Battn Hd Qrs at K.12.a.5.9

2. The Bath will parade at 1330 hours 9th inst to proceed by march route to KEIBERG. E.25.b. ROUTE. WESTHOEK SMITH ROAD BROODSEINDE Crossroads J.5.a.9.5. KIEBERG. Usual intervals between Coys. Coys will march in file. DRESS Battle order greatcoats rolled in waterproof sheets, Jerkins worn
On arrival at KEIBERG the Battn will halt for Teas, and rations for the 10th & 11th will be issued

3. Lewis Gun limbers. Water Cart and Mess Cart will report to Battn Hd Qrs at 10. am and Lewis Guns will be loaded at once. The Transport with one Cooker will then proceed in accordance with instructions issued to Transport Officer and will meet the Battn at KIEBERG at 3 pm

4. Arrangements for guides will be issued later

5. All Defence Schemes Air Photos, Intelligence, Work Policy S.A.A Trench Stores etc will be taken over and lists forwarded to Adjutant by 9 am 10th inst

6. Relief complete will be notified to Battn Hd Qrs by code message "ALL ABOARD"

7. The Q.M. will arrange for water to be brought up in Petrol Tins

8. Brigade Transport Lines will be situated on the road running N.E. from J.12.w.9.0 to J.6.d.u.1. and will move to new location on the 9th.

9. Tents and Shelters to be handed over to incoming Unit and receipt handed to Adjutant on arrival at KEIBERG.

10. Instructions for the transport of Officers kits and Blankets to the rear will be issued later

11. The camp will be left in a clean and sanitary condition and certificates to the effect handed to the Adjutant on parade

Lieut
Adjt 2 Leinster Regt

OPERATION ORDER No 37

Re: Sheet 28NE, 6000   10th Oct 1918

1. The 109 Inf Bde (36 Div) will relieve the 88th Inf Battalion that portion of the line between the present Southern Boundary and L.13 b y y on the night 10th/11th October.

2. The Batn will hold the front from HEULEBEEK (exclusive) to the Northern Divisional Boundary.

3. The disposition of the Batn will be as follows:
RIGHT Coy — B Coy from the HEULEBEEK exclusive to the Station exclusive.
LEFT Coy — A Coy from the Station inclusive to the Northern Divisional Boundary
SUPPORT Coy — 'C' Coy will remain in Support
RESERVE — The two platoons of D Coy now relieved by A Coy will return to D Coy in Reserve and take over original positions as taken over from the Royal Fusiliers.

4. A Coy HQ will arrange to share HQ with B Coy on L.8 a b y.

5. O.C. B Coy will take over post held by A Coy north of the HEULEBEEK.

6. The Front Line Coys will each arrange to have one platoon in close support.

Continued

2. Relief will take place as soon as darkness allows.

3. Completion of relief to be reported by code word SHUNT.

OPERATION ORDER No 38.
By
Lt Col H.C. Weldon Comdg 2nd Leinster Regt.

Ref Map 28NE Locre.   11 Oct 1915

1. The 2nd Leinster Regt will be relieved in the line on the night of 11th/12th Oct by the 2nd South Wales Borderers.

2. Guides (as already detailed) will report to 2/O Battn at Batln HQ at 1730 hours.
   A Coy 2 Leinster Regt will be relieved by   B Coy South W Borderers
   B   A
   C   D
   D   C

3. All Barrel Stores, defence schemes, Bar Chart Intelligence, CAR, trench latrine etc will be handed over and original copy forwarded to O Room by 12.00 hours on 12th inst.

4. On completion of relief the Battn will move into support in the BECELAERE area in square K.7.a. The Quartermaster will arrange to have all tents and shelters in this Camp and forward several receipts to O Room.

5. The following routes to the new Camp will be taken the 2nd Hampshire Regt will first — will be followed K.13.a.5.9 – K.8.a.4.2 – K.11.3.2 – K.11.7 to K.11.c.1.2 POTTERIJE BRUG K.7.a.

6. Junior Coy Leaders and Officers thereof will be at Batln HQ by 1830 hours. The Mess Cart and Mates Cart will report at Batln HQ at 1900 hours. Empty petrol tins taken from by one L Division only or less four tanks.

7. Coy Commanders to report at Batln HQ in person when passing after relief.

8. Completion of relief to be reported to Bn HQ by code word DOROTHY.

9. Arrival in new camp to be reported to Adjutant.

10. Sentries will be acquainted of their duties by code word — KAJEMA

                                            A D Myr
                                            Lieut
                                            Adjt 2 Leinster Regt

OPERATION ORDERS No.39.   Copy No... 2
by
Lieut. Colonel. H.W.Weldon., Commanding 2nd. Battalion Leinster Regiment.
Ref: Special Tactical Map "A"   13.10.1918.
....

(1)   The 88th. Inf. Brigade will attack the enemy on the 14th. October at Zero hour - to be notified later - with the 86th. Brigade on its left & the 109th. Brigade on its right -
For
    (a) Inter Brigade Boundaries.
    (b) Objectives.
    (c) Barrage Time Table.
    (d) Liaison Posts with Flank Brigades.
See SPECIAL MAP.

(2)   The 88th. Infantry Brigade will carry out the attack under an intense artillery barrage.

1st. Phase. - The 2nd. Leinster Regiment will advance at ZERO hour & capture the first objective, which is the limit of the Field Artillery Barrage. The objective is the line marked on the Map running through - L.12.a. - L.12.c. - L.18.a.
"A" Company will be the right front company.
"C"   "   "   "   "   " left front company.
"B"   "   will attack on the left of "C" Coy, the whole of "B" Coy being N. of the HEULBEEK. - "D" Company will be in Reserve.

(3)   On arrival at MARY BRIDGE (L.9.c.6.6.) the whole of "B" Coy will cross the bridge - One platoon will remain S. of the HEULBEEK, on the left of "C" Company & will be under the orders of O.C. "C" Company. "D" Coy will move into Support & "B" Coy (less one platoon) into reserve. -

(4)   After the capture of the 1st. Objective at Zero plus 1 hour 55 minutes, the barrage will halt from plus 1 hour 55 minutes - to plus 2 hours 12 minutes - During this halt the 4th. Worcester Regt. will move up into position to carry on the advance under a heavy artillery barrage which will move at the rate of 1000 yards in two minutes. -

(5)   During the attack "B" Company (and after passing MARY BRIDGE one platoon of "B" Company) will be responsible for guarding the left flank of the Brigade.
     "A" Coy will have a strong platoon on its right flank to guard the right flank of the Brigade.

(6)   Bridges (for the purpose of crossing the HEULBEEK) will be allotted at the position of assembly as under :-
    "A" Company - 7 Bridges.
    "C"   "   - 7   "
    "B"   "   - 2   "
These will be carried by men of the 2nd. Hants & 1st/2nd. Monmouths & will be under the orders of the respective O.C.Companies.

(7)   Immediately the 1st. Objective is captured the Battalion will at once reorganize so that it will be ready to move forward again when required.

(8)   The O.C. Attacking Companies will be responsible for establishing Liason Posts with the flank brigades at the positions shown on the attached Map "A"

(9)   It should be noted that the Advance is due East on a Compass bearing of 102°

(10)   Every opportunity should be taken to make use of Visual Signalling. The Brigade Signal Section will be constantly on the alert to pick up Stations.
     Strips and POPHAM Panels should be taken.

(II) **Dropping of Supplies.** - The following arrangements will be in force during the operations for dropping ammunition, pigeons and rations by aeroplane in case of urgent necessity.

The following signals will be made by use of ground strips to call for any of the above :-

    (a) <u>Bundle Packed Ammunition</u> - "V"

    (b) <u>Machine Gun Ammunition</u> - "M"

    (c) <u>Pigeons</u> - ☐ (a square)

    (d) <u>Food and Rations</u> - "F"

Attention will be called to the signals by the lighting of a WHITE ground flare or the firing of a WHITE VERY LIGHT.

(I2) <u>Contact Aeroplanes</u>

    (a) The attacking troops will carry RED FLARES, Discs, and American Cloth on Box Respirators, for the purpose of communicating with contact aeroplanes.

    (b) These and every other practicable means of signalling their position will be used by the attacking troops at :-

        (1) Zero plus 1 hour 20 minutes.
        (2) Zero plus 3 hours,

and at such times as called for by the contact aeroplanes.

    (c) The contact aeroplanes will call for signals from the attacking troops by sounding a KLAXON Horn and dropping WHITE Lights.

    (d) The contact aeroplane will be marked with TWO BLACK RECTANGULAR FLAGS (2 ft by 1 ft 3 inches) attached to and projecting from the lower plane on each side of the fuselage and each contact aeroplane will also have a TRAILING STREAMER. All troops are to be warned how to recognise a contact aeroplane.

                                  Lieut.
                      Adjt. 2nd. Battalion Leinster Regt.

Issued at ....

<u>DISTRIBUTION.</u>

    Copy No. 1.   O.C.
              2.   Adjutant.
              3.   O.C. "A" Coy.
              4.   O.C. "B" "
              5.   O.C. "C" "
              6.   O.C. "D" "
              7.   R.T.O.
              8.   Quartermaster.
              9.   R.S.M.
            10.   Signalling Officer.
            11.   Intelligence Officer.
            12.   88th. Inf. Bde. H.Q.
            13.   Medical Officer.
            14.   War Diary.
            15.   File.

OPERATION ORDERS No 40.

by
Lieut Colonel H. W. Weldon, Commanding 2nd Leinster Regt.
FRIDAY 25.10.1918

Reference Sheet 29

(1) The Battalion will move tomorrow 26th inst. to an area W. of MOUSCRON by Route March.

(2) Companies will march independently to the Battalion Starting point (Fork Roads M.28.c.5.8) assembling there at 08.00 hrs from whence they will march in the following order:—
  "A" Coy, "B, C, D" at 100 yards interval.

(3) DRESS:— Battle Order with Greatcoats rolled and Carried, pouches, haversacks. Steel helmets will be worn.— Recent drafts will carry their packs.

(4) Blankets (rolled in bundles of 10) Officers kits, & Mess Gear to be stacked outside billets by 7 a.m.

(5) Transport will accompany Battalion with interval of 25 yards between each six vehicles.

(6) Advance billeting party, consisting of 2/Lieut McMahon & C.Q.M.S. and 1 N.C.O. per Coy. will report with bicycles at STACKEGHEM CHURCH at 5–15 a.m.

(7) Present billets will be left in a Scrupulously Clean and Sanitary State & certificate to this effect handed to Adjutant at Starting Point by each Coy. 1 O.R. per Company for handing over will report with kits at 8 AM to Capt Harstell

(8) Arrival in new billets to be reported to Adjutant.

R. A. Ashford Capt.
Adjt 2nd Leinster Regiment

DISTRIBUTION:
Copy No 1. C.O.
  2. 2nd in command.
  3. Adjutant
  4. O.C. "A" Coy
  5. O.C. "B" "
  6. O.C. "C" "
  7. O.C. "D" "
  8. Quartermaster
  9. R.T.O.
  10. R.S.M.
  11. FILE
  12. WAR DIARY.

Op Or 96

ADMINISTRATIVE ORDER No.1.   Copy No. 2
                                    by
Lieut. Colonel. H.W.Weldon., Commanding 2nd. Battalion Leinster Regt.
In the field.   13.10.1918.

(1)   Rations for 14th. inst. will be issued in this Camp & will
     be carried on the man. Every man will march out of this Camp with
     a full water bottle. It should be explained to the men that these
     rations & water must last till the night of the 14th. inst.

(2)   The following will be stacked by the road side by 4 p.m.
     Officers Kits, Blankets (bundles of 10), Greatcoats (packed by sections)

(3)   Only 12 L.G.Magazines per gun will be taken into action.
              64 magazines per Company will be stacked on the roadside
     near the Cookers by 4 p.m.
              32 magazines per Company will be brought up with rations
     on the night of the 14th. inst. & 32 per Company on the night of the
     15th. inst.

(4)   RUM will not be issued in this Camp, but will be carried to
     the position of assembly & issued just before dawn.

(5)   All Lewis Guns & 12 magazines per gun will be stacked in
     limbers by 3 p.m. The Lewis Guns will move under the orders of
     the R.T.O. & will be unloaded as the Battalion arrives at the
     SHRINE at K.12.a.70.75.
              At this point Companies will also take up shovels as under :-
                 "A" Company.   - 48
                 "B"   "   - 48
                 "C"   "   - 48
                 "D"   "   - 46
                 H.Q.   - 20
              The Lewis Guns, magazines and shovels will be stacked by the
     roadside by Companies and there must be no delay at this point.

(6)   The Battalion will parade at 1710 hours today in BATTLE ORDER
     to march to position of assembly - Order of March -
              H.Q. - "A" - "C" - "B" - "D" -
              Route (which 2nd. Hants will picket) - K.7.d.2.7.- K.14.a.5.8.
     -K.9.b.8.8. - bridge at K.10.b.1.7.- K.11.a.65.30.- Shrine at
     K.12.a.70.75. - K.12.b.05.45. - thence to track to K.12.b.65.30.
              At this point the Battalion will be met by Guides, who will
     conduct Companies to the vicinity of Raymond Farm.
(7)   All Officers will report to the Signalling Officer at 4.45 p.m.
     in order to Synchronize watches.

                                                    [signature]
                                                            Lieut.
                         Adjt. 2nd. Battalion Leinster Regiment.

DISTRIBUTION.
   Copy No. 1.   C.O.
            2.   Adjutant.
            3.   O.C."A" Coy.
            4.   O.C."B" "
            5.   O.C."C" "
            6.   O.C."D" "
            7.   R.T.O.
            8.   Quartermaster.
            9.   R.S.M.
           10.   Intelligence Officer.
           11.   Signalling Officer.
           12.   Medical Officer.
           13.   88th. Inf. Bde. H.Q.
           14.   File.

CONFIDENTIAL

WAR DIARY

of

2nd Battalion The Leinster Regiment.

From 1st November To 30th November, 1918.

(VOLUME NO.8).

WAR DIARY
or
INTELLIGENCE SUMMARY.
(Erase heading not required.)

Army Form 2118.

November. 2nd Kensington Regt.

Place	Date	Hour	Summary of Events and Information	Remarks and references to Appendices
Field	1st		The G.O.C. 15th Corps inspected the 86th Brigade at CROIX in the afternoon. After the march past he complimented the Brigade on its turn-out and drill and expressed his appreciation of the fact that by the Battn. in the FLANDERS operations. Maj. Gen. Sir H. B. Little was by Maj. Gen. CAYLEY cmg. 29th Div. 2/Lt W. H. BARKER M.C. and 2/Lt S. COLE away for hospital and leave respectively. 74175 Sgt ? HARLON was awarded the Croix de Guerre.	
	2nd		Coy. Training.	
	3rd		Bn. Parade for Divine Service as under: B. Cs. 0900 hours. CROIX Church. C. of E's. 1100 hours. English Church. CROIX. Non-Conformists. and Presbyts. 1015. Biscuiterie. CROIX	
	4th		Coy. Training.	
	5th		Coy. Training.	

WAR DIARY
or
INTELLIGENCE SUMMARY

Army Form 2118.

2nd Lincolnshire Regt

Place	Date	Hour	Summary of Events and Information	Remarks and references to Appendices
	6		29th Divn. moved to E. of to Corps Area. Coming under the orders of G.O.C. Corps. The Bn. proceeded by march route to area 29 T.3 and to area ROUBAIX - MOUSCRON - TOMBROEK, any billets. Hun got the right. Major T.R. FREND D.S.O. left to become 2nd i/c Comd. of 2nd Hants. Capt. V.J. FARRELL D.S.O. M.C. took command of the Bn. on the temporary absence of Lt. Col. WEDDY on leave.	MM
	7		Bn. took over the front line in the BOSSUYT area from 2/16 London Regt. from 29 U.24.d.6.3 to V.14.d.o.o. Dispositions: C coy (front line) U.28.d 2 V.13.c, B (support) in billets at U.10.G. D coy (Reserve) 032 B.H.Q. at 032.d.8.0. A coy (Reserve) in 033.	M
	8		Bn. in front line. In the evg. C coy. crossed the SCHELDT and grand COURANTE Rivers (these in flood) encountering no opposition. By dawn on 9— the II coy. who established in the villages to L'ESPINOIS. Patrols sent out. The enemy had left at 09.00 hours the F— after blowing up	MM

WAR DIARY
or
INTELLIGENCE SUMMARY.
(Erase heading not required.)

Army Form C.2118.

2nd Leinster Regt

Place	Date	Hour	Summary of Events and Information	Remarks and references to Appendices
all road junctions	9	6	Bn. followed up the enemy slowly but failed to gain contact. By 1500 hours we had reached the Bns 3d/E26 – 2d – 9c – 16b – 16d – 22b – 22d – 28a. Bns then the forward troops. The enemy was pushed forward leaving behind the locality in all about 12 hours before he reached it.	W
	10.		The 2nd Hants relieving the present and Hy. Bn. pushed into support. The Hants were trying to gain contact although the enemy was previously last. Bn. marched forward to ST. SAVEUR halting there for the night.	W
	11.		ARMISTICE DAY. Bn. on the line outside of the armistice was that the hostilities (ended) by 1100 hours were to be the front line. Bn twelve (forced) with all ranks to A. Mercation lay in front. By a lucky exhibit the G.O.C. 86 Bde. with a few country men drove	W

Army Form C. 2118.

WAR DIARY
or
INTELLIGENCE SUMMARY.
(Erase heading not required.)

2nd Leinster Regt

Place	Date	Hour	Summary of Events and Information	Remarks and references to Appendices
TOURNAI		5	The Grey of the River DENDRE at LESSINES. Our Troops are in comfort of retiring with the greatest enthusiasm. Our Bn. was at TOURNAI 1.4.44.118	Mr
			at 1100 hrs. Bn proceeded to NODEEG to billets.	
	12.		Bn. Marched to NODEEG. The following awards were made:—	
			D.S.O. Lt Col. H.W. WELDON. Cnj. 2-3 LEINSTER REGT.	
			Bar to M.M. 2504 Pte J.J. RICE.	
			M.M. 3875 Sgt T. HOEY. 4455. Pte. A. DONOVAN. 1831 Sgt G. KILLIKELLY Scar..	
			3617 Pte J. NOLAN. 4292 Sgt. T. MALONEY. 15389 Pte. R. CLARKE. 10924 Pte. F. McARDLE.	
			4582 L/c A. O'NEILL. 15310. Pte. W. McKNIGHT. 16270. Cpl. J. GERRD. 2350. Cpl. T. McCORMICK.	
			5436. Pte. W. BURTON. 8776. Cpl. J. GREEN. 2987. Cpl. T. BRENNAN.	Mr
			8826. Sgt. T. BROWN. 4831. Pte. H. JENNIS. 10912 Pte. D. CORRISS.	
			4257. Pte. J. BANNON.	Mr
	13.		Bn. Marched to LESSINES where it was billeted.	

WAR DIARY
or
INTELLIGENCE SUMMARY.

(Erase heading not required.) 2nd Leinster Regt

Army Form C.2118.

Place	Date	Hour	Summary of Events and Information	Remarks and references to Appendices
LESSINES	14.		Bn. at LESSINES. Lt. Col. H.S. WELDON D.S.O. returned from leave. B. Coy took over outpost system at DEUX ACREN from 30th Division.	Ap1
	15.		Bn. at LESSINES. 240 all ranks form a Brigade Ceremonial Parade. R.C's for this purpose attend a Patriotic Mass and Te Deum held in honour of Maj. ALBERT 1st in St. PIERRE Church	Ap2
LESSINES	16.		Coy training. D Coy reliefs B Coy in the outpost portion	Ap3
	17.		Bn. paraded for Church as usual. R.C's at Church. LESSINES at 10.30 hrs. Prot'ts and the Conformists at EGLISE COMMUNALE LESSINES at 10.00 hrs. Other 2 Lettres Biroux. D Coy in outpost portion.	Ap4
	18.		9h 29' Bn. standing to find at this all in force to receive the RH.M.L. works	Ap5

WAR DIARY or INTELLIGENCE SUMMARY

Army Form C.2118.

2nd Leinster Regt

Place	Date	Hour	Summary of Events and Information	Remarks and references to Appendices
R.P.			4th Bn. marched via Bois de Zetrud and Bassilly to Enghien. Distance 15 kilos.	M
TOURNAI	19.		Bn. in ENGHIEN. Coy. Training. 9/Lt R.J. KELLY joined from 4th Bn.	M
BRUSSELS	20.		Bn. in ENGHIEN. Coy. Training.	M
	21.		4th Divn. today the march continued and the Bn marched to BRAINE-LE-CHATEAU via SAINTES and TUBIZE. 2d Bn. billets in BRAINE-LE-CHATEAU. A Company (Coy) it appears as the 1st are under Capt. V.J. FARRELL D.S.O. M.C. marches to HALS and SAINTES to bring Home for GANSHOREN (5 km. N. of BRUSSELS) billeting there for the night.	F M
	22.		Bn. in Hd.Qrs. 4 Coys Company marched to the Lamb JORDAINS to KING ALBERT and his Allies and his Minister the Duke's, Staff into BRUSSELS. KING ALBERT	M

WAR DIARY
or
INTELLIGENCE SUMMARY.

(Erase heading not required.)

2nd Lincolns Regt.

Army Form C.2118.

Place	Date	Hour	Summary of Events and Information	Remarks and references to Appendices
Brussels			indescribable enthusiasm. the streets being thronged with people cheering wildly. King ALBERT took the salute at the House of Parliament. The Bn. marched off to the GRENADIER BARRACKS having drawn tins at 1600 hours.	
			The (C) Coy entered at 1800. Coy ex refreshed the Bn. at BRAINE-LE-CHATEAU.	M.W.
	23.		Bn. left by Diesel Guides for KT.HQ. BDE. Bn marches to OHAIN via WATERLOO. Lay the first British Battalion to pass over the field of WATERLOO since the fight 1815. Bn Hd. Qrs. and HMKs at OHAIN	M.W.
Ohain	24.		Bn. at OHAIN. In following awards were made: Bar to M.C. Capt. T.F. MacKeehan C.F. M.C. M.C. Capt. T. Moran. Lt. Owen-Norris R.A.M.C. 2/Lt. H. Wilde Capt. B.E. Sanders. Lt. D. Hickey	M.W.
	25.		Bn. Marched to OTTIGNIES via St. LAMBERT-CEROUX-MOUSTY. Bn. into billets at STYMON.	

Army Form C.118.

WAR DIARY
or
INTELLIGENCE SUMMARY.
(Erase heading not required.)

2nd Leinster Regt.

Place	Date	Hour	Summary of Events and Information	Remarks and references to Appendices
	26.		Bn. at OTTIGNIES. Coy. Training.	
Ru.F. 6 Brussels	27.		Bn. marched via COURT-ST-ETIENNE – HEVILLERS – WALHAIN-ST-PAUL to Sart-les-Walhain where it was billeted for the night.	M
	28.		Bn. marched via ORBAIS – PERWEZ – Gd. ROSIERE – ECHEELE to HARRET where it was billeted for the night.	M
	29.		Bn. marched via FORVILLE – LAVOIR to MOHA where it was billeted for the night.	M
LIEGE 7 Mortier 9	30		Bn. marched via HUY (where it crossed the MEUSE) – STREE – SENY to OUFFET (Lake part of Girece C.H.Q.) where it was billeted for the night.	M

Muller Lieut-Colonel
Commanding 2nd Bn Leinster Regt.

Operation Order No. 40   Copy No. 12

Reference Map Sheet 29   7/11/18

I The Battn will take over the front line from V.24.d.6.3 to V.14.d.0.0 on the night 7-8 November relieving two Coys 2/16 LONDON REGT.

II On completion of relief dispositions will be as follows.
Front line   C Coy in U.28.d. & V.13.c.
Support   B Coy in Billets U.10.b
Reserve   A   O.33
              D   O.32

Battalion H.Qrs.   O.32.a.9.0

III Battalion will rendezvous at Sok Roads T.5.b.3.6. at 2.30 p.m.
Guides for B & C Coys will meet Coys at U.11.a.0.6. at 5 p.m.

IV Advance parties of 1 Officer per Coy & 1 N.C.O per platoon for B & C Coys will proceed to U.6.a.3.5 obtaining necessary information from H.Qrs of 2/16 LONDON REGT and reconnoitering positions of Coys.
Parties of A & D proceed to take over billets as arranged.

V Dress Battle Order (men will wear overcoats and carry one blanket per man). Packs and remaining blankets to be ready for transport at 11 a.m. also Officers kits and surplus mess gear (dumped on arrival Mairie Q.M.)

VI Lewis Gun Limbers and cookers will proceed with Coys (except C) carrying rations for 8th inst.

VII Transport lines & Q.M. Stores will remain as at present.

VIII Any dose of ammunition etc. that exists will be taken over and location and size of dump reported at once to Battn H.Qrs.

IX Completion of relief by B & C Coys to be reported by runner. A & D Coys will report present in billets.

                                      (SD) F H WHITEHEAD Captain
                                                Adjutant

Operation Order N° 41   Copy N° 12

Ref. Map Tournay & Brussels 1:100000   17th November 1918

1. The 29th Division will advance tomorrow, 18th inst. as part of the Allied Force to occupy territory evacuated by the enemy.

2. The 88th Bde Group will move by route march to ENGHIEN.

3. The Battalion will parade outside Orderly Room at 08.50 hrs in "Full Marching Order".
   Order of march: Hd Qrs, A, B, C, D, Transport.

4. Intervals - 30 yards between Battalions, 10 yards between Companies, 5 yards between platoons - 10 yards between rear Company and Transport.

5. Blankets (tightly rolled in bundles of 10) to be stacked outside billets at 0400 hrs. Officers Kits and Mess Gear at Q.M Stores or Orderly Room (whichever nearest) at 07.30 hrs.

6. Advance Party of 4 C.Q.M.S., 1 N.C.O for Hd Qrs, & Transport under 2/Lt McMahon will report at Orderly Room at 6.30 am.

7. Present billets to be left in a scrupulously clean condition and certificate rendered on parade.

8. Arrival in billets and position of picquets (if any) to be reported to ~~Orderly Room~~ Adjutant.

                                              A H Whitmore
                                                    Captain
                                   Adjutant 2nd Leinster Regiment

DISTRIBUTION.
Copy No 1   C.O.
        2   2nd in Command
        3   Adjutant
        4   OC 'A' Coy
        5   OC 'B' Coy
        6   OC 'C' Coy
        7   OC 'D' Coy
        8   R.T.O
        9   Quartermaster
       10   R.S.M
       11   88th Bde HQ
       12   War Diary
       13   File

Operation Orders "42"   Copy N°. 12

Lt. Col. H.S. Weldon. D.S.O. by Comdg. 2nd Bn. Leinster Regt.

Ref. Map. BRUSSELS.   20th November 1918

1. The advance EAST will be continued tomorrow 21st inst. The Battn. will march to Billets in BRAME LE CHATEAU Area.

2. Parade outside "A" & "B" Coy. billets at 09.25 hrs. in the following order H.Qrs. "B", "C", "D", "A" Transport. Dress. Full Marching Order.

3. Lewis Gun limbers and Pack animals will follow their respective Coys.

4. Blankets (tightly rolled in 10's) to be stacked outside billets at 08.00 hrs. Officers kits and Mess Gear. outside Coy. billets at 08.30 hrs.

5. Advance Party (composition as usual) to report to 2/Lt. McMAHON at Orderly Room with bicycles at 07.00 hrs.

6. Present billets to be left in a scrupulously clean & sanitary condition and usual certificate rendered on parade.

7. Arrival in billets and position of picquets (if any) to be reported to Adjutant.

"D" Coy. find the inlying picquet.

Distribution.
1. C.O
2. 2nd in Command.
3. Adjutant
4. O.C. "A" Coy.
5. — "B" —
6. — "C" —
7. — "D" —
8. R.T.O
9. Q.M.
10. R.S.M.
11. 88th Inf. Bde. H.Q.
12. File
13. War Diary.

A.H. Whitehead
Captain
Adjt. 2nd Bn. Leinster Regt.

Operation Order No. 43.   Copy No. 13

Lt. Col. H. W. Weldon. D.S.O. by Commanding 2nd Battn. Leinster Regt.

Ref Map. BRUSSELS. 6   22.11.18

1. The advance EAST will be continued tomorrow 23rd inst. — The Battn. will march to billets in OHAIN Area.

2. The Battn. will provide the Advanced Guard to the 88th Brigade Group. — Dispositions of Detachments forming Advanced Guard will be found on attached march table.

3. The Battn. will parade outside Orderly Room in the following order at 08.30 hours, C, D, A, B. H.Q. Coy. Transport. Dress:- Full marching order.

4. Lewis Gun limbers and Pack animals will follow respective Coys. "C" Coy. Cookers will follow the Company.

5. Blankets (tightly rolled in 10's) to be stacked outside billets at 07.00 hrs. — Officers Kits & Mess Gear outside Coy. billets at 07.30 hours.

6. Advance Party (composed as usual) to report to 2 Lt. McMAHON at Orderly Room at 07.00 hours with bicycles.

7. Present billets to be left in a scrupulously clean & sanitary condition and usual certificate rendered on parade.

8. Arrival in billets and position of picquets (if any) to be reported to Adjutant. ("B" Coy. find inlying picquet.).

DISTRIBUTION
1. C.O.
2. 2nd in Command.
3. Adjutant.
4. O.C. "A" Coy.
5. -- "B" -
6. -- "C" -
7. -- "D" -
8. R.T.O.
9. Q.M.
10. R.S.M.
11. 88th Inf. Bde.
12. File.
13. War Diary.

A H Whitehead
Captain.
for. O.C. Comdg. 2nd Bn. Leinster Regt.

Operation Order N° 44   Copy N° 12

Lt. Col. H. W. WELDON. D.S.O. by Commanding 2nd Battn. Leinster Regt.

Ref. Sheet BRUSSELS 6.   26.11.18.

1. The Advance EAST will be continued tomorrow 27th inst. — the Battn. will march to billets in the WALHAIN ST. PAUL Area —

2. The Battn. will parade at 09.30 hours opposite Orderly Room in the following order H.Q. A, B, C, D, Coy. Transport. —

3. Lewis Gun limbers and Pack animals will accompany respective Coys. —

4. Advance Party (as usual) will report to 2LT. McMAHON at Orderly Room at 06.00 hours —

5. Blankets (in bundles of 10) to be stacked outside Orderly Room at 08.00 hours. Officers Kits & Mess Gear at 08.30 hours. —

6. Present billets to be left in a scrupulously clean state — Usual certificate on parade —

7. Arrival in new billets to be reported to Adjutant.

DISTRIBUTION
1. C.O.
2. 2nd in Command.
3. Adjutant.
4. O.C. "A" Coy.
5. — "B" Coy.
6. — "C" Coy.
7. — "D" Coy
8. R.T.O.
9. Q.M.
10. R.S.M.
11. 88th Inf. Bde.
12. File.
13. War Diary.

(SD) A. H. WHITEHEAD. Captain.
Adjutant. 2nd Bn. Leinster Regt.

Operation Orders No. 45.
by
Lt. Col. W. H. WELDON. D.S.O. Commanding 2nd Battn. Leinster Regt.

Copy No 13

Ref. Sheet. BRUSSELS. 6.   27. 11. 18.

1. The advance EAST will be continued tomorrow 28th inst. The Battn. will march to billets at HANRET.

2. The Battn. will parade on main road with head of column opposite Orderly Room at 09.20 hours in the following order:— A, B, C, D, H.Qrs. Transport.

3. Blankets (neatly rolled in 10's) to be stacked outside Company billets at 08.00 hours. Officers kits and Mess Gear at 08.30 hours.
   1 Guide per Coy. for lorries to report at Q.M. Stores at 07.45 hours.

4. Advance Party (as usual) to report to 2 Lt. McMAHON at Orderly Room at 07.30 hours.

5. Present billets to be left in a scrupulously clean condition. Usual certificate on parade.

6. The usual clock halts to be observed except that the column will halt from 12.40 hrs to 13.00 hrs.

7. Arrival in billets to be reported to Adjutant.

DISTRIBUTION
1. C.O.
2. 2nd in Command
3. Adjutant
4. O.C. 'A' Coy
5. " 'B' Coy
6. " 'C' Coy
7. " 'D' Coy
8. R.T.O
9. Q.M.
10. R.S.M.
11. 88th Inf. Bde.
12. File
13. War Diary.

(SD) A. H. WHITEHEAD Captain.
Adjutant 2nd Battn. Leinster Regt.

Operation Orders No. 46.
by
Lt. Col. H.W. WELDON. D.S.O. Comdg. 2nd Battn. Leinster Regt.

Ref. Sheet. BRUSSELS. 6 - LIEGE. 7.   28.11.1918.

Copy. No. 73

1. The advance EAST will be continued tomorrow 29th inst. The Battn. will march to billets at MOHA.

2. The Battn. will parade on Road opposite Church HANRET (at right angles to Main Road) with head of column just clear of Main Road at 09.15 hrs. in the following order, B, C, D, H.Qrs. A. Transport.
The Main Road is to be left clear until 4th Worcesters & 2nd Hants have passed.

3. Blankets (neatly rolled in 10's) to be stacked outside Company Billets at 07.45 hrs. Officers kits & Mess Gear at 08.15 h. 1 Guide per Company for lorries to report to Q.M. Stores at 07.30 hours.

4. Advance Parties (as usual) to report to 2 LT. McMAHON at Orderly Room at 07.00 hours.

5. The usual clock hour halt to be observed except that the column will halt from 12.30 hrs to 13.00 hrs.

6. Present Billets to be left in a scrupulously clean state - Usual certificate on parade.

7. Arrival in billets and number of men falling out on march to be reported to Adjutant.

DISTRIBUTION
1. C.O
2. 2nd in Command
3. Adjutant
4. O.C. A. Coy.
5. " B Coy.
6. " C Coy
7. " D
8. R.T.O
9. Q.M.
10. R.S.M.
11. 88th Inf. Bde.
12. File
13. War Diary.

(SD) A.H. WHITEHEAD. Captain
Adjutant 2nd Bn. Leinster Regt.

Operation Orders No. 47
by
Lt. Col. H.W. WELDON. D.S.O. Comdg. 2nd Battn. Leinster Regt.

Ref. Sheet LIEGE 7 & MARCHE. Q.   29.11.18

1. The advance EAST will be continued tomorrow 30th inst. The Battn. will march to billets at OUFFET.

2. The Battn. will parade on Road running SOUTH from MOHA. (head of column 400 yards S. of A in MOHA) in the following order C, D, H.Q, A, B, Transport at 07.15 hours. Transport except L. Gun Limbers and pack animals will proceed Brigaded from Brigade starting point).

3. Blankets (rolled in 10's) to be stacked outside Coy. Billets at 06.30 hours. Officers Kits & Mess Gear at 06.30 hours. 1 Guide per Coy for lorries to report to Q.M. Stores at 06.30 hours.

4. Advance Party (as usual) to report at Orderly Room at 06.30 hours.

5. Present billets to be left in a scrupulously clean state. Usual certificate on parade.

6. Usual clock-hour halts except from 12.40 hours to 13.00 hours.

7. Arrival in Billets and number of men falling out on march to be reported to Adjutant.

DISTRIBUTION
1. C.O
2. 2nd in Command
3. Adjutant
4. O.C. 'A' Coy.
5. " 'B' Coy.
6. " 'C' Coy.
7. " 'D' Coy.
8. R.T.O.
9. Q.M.
10. R.S.M.
11. 88th Inf. Bde.
12. File.
13. War Diary.

(SD) A.H. WHITEHEAD. Captain.
Adjt. 2nd Bn. Leinster Regt.

Operation Orders No 48   Copy No 11
by
Lieut. Col. H.W. Weldon. DSO. Comdg 2nd Battn Leinster Regt

Sheet MARCHE 9   30. 11. 1918.

1. The advance EAST will be continued tomorrow Dec 1st. The Battn will march to billets at AYWAILLE

2. The Battn will parade at 09.15 hrs opposite A.S.C. Corps Billets. in the following order. D. HdQrs ABC Transport

3. Blankets (in bundles of 10) to be stacked outside Coy Billets at 07.00 hours. Officers Kits & Mess Gear at 08.00 hours. 1 Guide per Coy for lorries to report at Batt Stores at 07.00 hrs

4. Advance Party (as usual) to report at Orderly Room at 06.30 hrs

5. Present billets to be left in a scrupulously clean state - usual certificate on parade -

6. Usual clock halts to be observed except from 12.30 to 13.00 hrs when haversack ration will be consumed.

7. Arrival in billets and number of men falling out on march to be reported to Adjutant

(Sd) A H Whitehead Captain
Adjutant 2nd Bn Leinster Regt

DISTRIBUTION
1. CO
2. 2nd in Command
3. Adjutant
4. OC 'A' Coy
5. OC 'B' "
6. OC 'C' "
7. OC 'D' "
8. R.T.O
9. Q.M
10. R.S.M
11. 88th Inf Bde
12. War Diary
13. File

CONFIDENTIAL

WAR DIARY

of

2nd Battalion The Leinster Regiment

From 1st December To 31st December, 1918.

(VOLUME NO.9)

WAR DIARY for December 1918
INTELLIGENCE SUMMARY

2nd Lincoln Regt.

Army Form C. 2118.

Place	Date	Hour	Summary of Events and Information	Remarks and references to Appendices
	1st		Bn. marched to AWAN via COMBLAIN-FAIROU-AUTOUR-AYWAILLE.	No
Of AWAN	2nd		Bn rested at AWAN	
AWAN	3rd		Bn paraded for Divine Service (C.of E.) at the Chateau chapel at 10.00 hours. Company Training for the rest of the morning.	No
	4th		Bn marched to billets in the BELLEVAUX - JOHOSTE ROD (CLABREDand) via MOULE and SOUGNE	No
M.L.	5th		The Bn marched to MALMEDY forming up for SPA entering the Armistice Comm. at 1.00 via thro' FRANCOCHAMPS, crossing the frontier at 13.55 hours.	No
BEFORE GERMAN	6th		2nd Bn Durhams to attack in spring marching over bridges to NIEDERS.	No

Army Form C. 2118.

WAR DIARY
or
INTELLIGENCE SUMMARY
(Erase heading not required.)

2nd Leinster Regt

Place	Date	Hour	Summary of Events and Information	Remarks and references to Appendices
A+B	7"		Bn. Marched via ELSENBORN - KALTER HERBERG - MONTJOIE to	
In the field Germany			KONZEN, billeting there for the night.	M
	8"		Bn. Marched to VLATTEN via SCHMIDT and HEIMBACH, billeting there for the night.	M
	9"		Battalion marched to ERP via SOLPICH and WEILER.	M
	10"		Bn. March to the eura tration area (FRECHEN) via KIERDORF and MORRATH. The billeting French escorts were issued to the officers and N.C.O.s.	M
	20"		CROIX DE GUERRE A L'ORDRE CORPS — Lt. Col. H.W. WELDON D.S.O.	M
			BRIGADE — Lt. M.G.E. SHARPE	
			MEDAILLE MILITAIRE — 2/140 Sgt. J. O'NEILL M.M.	M
			9/— V/M Men (not named) a Bar to his M.M.	M
			2504 Pte. J. RICE M.M. 18125 Pte. J. HALLIGAN M.M.	M

WAR DIARY

2nd Leicester Regt.

Army Form C. 2118.

Place	Date	Hour	Summary of Events and Information	Remarks and references to Appendices
Bn. at FRECHEN	11			
	12		Bn. paraded for Divine Service in winter. C of E at LUTHERAN CHURCH at 0900 hours. R.C's at R.C. CHURCH at 0915 hours.	M.L.
	13		The Bn. took part in the triumphal march through COLOGNE. The Divn. marched past Lt Gen TRAVERS cat II Corps with bayonets fixed and Colours, the RHINE by the HOHENZOLLERN bridge proceeding to MULHEIM when two telegrams were received. The following telegram from H.M. the KING to GEN SIR H. PLUMER cmdg. 2nd ARMY was received from Army functions. "I cannot trust FLANDERS without letting you know how very glad I am not to have been able to visit the 2nd ARMY, and personally to congratulate you on its triumph and during the past two days have watched with pride and Admiration the scenes of the famous	M.L.

WAR DIARY

Army Form C. 2118.

(Erase heading not required.) 5th Leinster Regt

Place	Date	Hour	Summary of Events and Information	Remarks and references to Appendices
			"Little with that the new M. the 2nd Army will only demonstrate" "Rest assured that I shall (with him & strat- the party now) meet of your Colours and trust that all ranks will soon be comfortably 39985 in their winter quarters. (2) GEORGE R.I.	
			The following message was received from Maj. Gen. Cavan 29 Div.	ℳ
			"Send to place on record my appreciation of the excellent work done by the Devon on the march to Colsene from 18th Nov to 10 Dec. The Bon. has been constantly marching with very little rest. The troops have frequently been kept on long but in spite of this its discipline maintains throat has been extremely	ℳ
		14/5	Bn. at MULHEIM. Lt. Vn. M.C.O.A. but Amm and his authority the M.O. 3211 Col. H. O'NEILL. 15069 Pte. W. WEBB. 18211 Pte. F. MARREN 10159 Pte. P. REILLY. 15456 Pte. G. B. WALKER	ℳ

(A9175) Wt W255/P360 600,000 12/17 D.D. & L. Sch Sta. Forms/C2118/15.

WAR DIARY

Army Form C. 2118.

1st Leinster Regt.

Place	Date	Hour	Summary of Events and Information	Remarks and references to Appendices
	15.		Bn. marched to ALTENBERG or ODENTHAL.	M/
	16.		Bn. marched to DHÜNN via STUMPF and DIRRHOUSEN. A Coy and D Coy was [billet] in DHÜNN. B Coy supply of a Platoon for outpost duty. C Coy provided HAZENBURG. Platoon found outpost duty. B Coy [march] to WERASLE KIRCHEN.	M/
	17.		Bn. rested	M/
	18.		B Coy [march] via DHÜNN to HÜLSEN blkty Hour. Coy. training	M/
	19.		Coy Training	M/
	20.		Coy Training. The VICTORIA CROSS was [awarded to]	M/

Army Form C. 2118.

WAR DIARY
~~INTELLIGENCE SUMMARY~~ 3rd Leinster Regt.
(Erase heading not required.)

Place	Date	Hour	Summary of Events and Information	Remarks and references to Appendices
			#119 Sgt. J. O'NEILL M.M. D coy and 18321 Pte. M. MOFFAT. D coy. for conspicuous gallantry and devotion to duty in October 1918.	Mos
	21.		Coy. Training	
	22.		Bn. paraded for Divine Service in buildings C.of.E. in LUTHERAN CHURCH at 0900 hours R.C.'s (B and C coys) at HÜLSERATHGEN - (A and D) at BHINN at 1000 hours	Mr
	23.		The Divisional Transport came to BHINN and offered a mens follst in local theatre.	Mr
	24.		Practical class - FRENCH, GERMAN & HINDUSTANI Was	Mr

Army Form C. 2118.

WAR DIARY

~~INTELLIGENCE SUMMARY~~

(Erase heading not required.)

2nd Leinster Regt.

Place	Date	Hour	Summary of Events and Information	Remarks and references to Appendices
	25.		Whit today, attack by about 100 Huns.	
			Bn. paraded for Divine Service in under CofE, RC's (Bat C) Lutheran Church shown at 0915. Hülsen (Bat C) at 0900 Hours. (A & J Bat H) Shown at 1800.	M
			Xmas Christmas Dinners in afternoon. Difficulties were LI at 1334 hours, and visited by Lt Col H.S.W. Monro DSO and Major Baker. Y/C Bakery. Pay Sergeants Non CoS with afternoon as gratuity.	
	26.		Bn. Bn. ast forces Labourhere in the morning. Coy was a inter Company TUG OF WAR. Bring Contest was held in the Evening.	M
	27.		Coy Training.	
	28.		Coy Training. Musketry. Officers Lectures ... Annual Thys to E.	

Army Form C. 2118.

WAR DIARY
or
~~Intelligence Summary~~ 2nd Leinster Regt

(Erase heading not required.)

Place	Date	Hour	Summary of Events and Information	Remarks and references to Appendices
	29.		T/2/Lt. L.M.J. PEARSONS Lt. A.E. NYE. Lt. (t/capt) E.J. KEMPE	M
			Bn. March to BROWS TOMBS on Mur. Ror.	
			C of E & LUTHERAN CHURCH at 0915 hours	M
			R.C.'s at B.HQ'RS at 0930 hours	
	30		Coy Training	
	31st		Bn. was allotted the batts at WERMELS KIRCHEN, there were no parades. Bn played 88 - F.A. and won by goals to nil. Evening a Coy	
	31st		Bn Colour party - Lt KIRKPATRICK M.C. 2/Lt. O'BRIEN mc Sgt. O'NEILL M.C.M.M. Sgt. MURPHY M.M. arrives back with the Battn Colours from BRR.	M

Malcolm F.M
m/ & Leinster Regt

(A9753) Wt W2358/P360 600,000 12/17 D. D. & L. Sch 53a. Forms/C2118/15.

SOUTHERN (LATE 29TH) DIVN
88TH INFY BDE

2ND BN LEINSTER REGT
JAN - JUN 1919

CONFIDENTIAL

WAR DIARY

of

2nd Battalion The Leinster Regiment.

From 1st January   To 31st January, 1919.

(VOLUME NO. 10).

****

WAR DIARY
or
INTELLIGENCE SUMMARY.
(Erase heading not required.)

2nd Leinster Regt.   January 1919

Place	Date	Hour	Summary of Events and Information	Remarks and references to Appendices
DHUNN	1st Jan 1919		Batn. in billets; ordinary parades carried on; At 1100 hours the Battn. paraded under the command of Lt-Col. H.W. Weldon D.S.O. Normally received the Colours which had arrived from BIRR. Afternoon devoted to Sports.	V.V.F.
DHUNN	2nd Jan 1919		Usual parades. Education classes (French, German, Mechanics English subjects) Carried out during the morning; Sports in the afternoon.	W.F.
DHUNN	3rd Jan 1919		The Usual Parades, Education Classes & Sports. The Corps Commander visited Classes at Education.	W.F.
DHUNN	4th Jan 1919		The Bn. paraded at 0930 hours to carry out a route march. Sport in the afternoon.	W.F.
DHUNN	5th Jan 1919		Usual Parades. Sports. Training Day. Of men teams trained by Sports Officer.	W.F.

WAR DIARY
or
INTELLIGENCE SUMMARY.

(Erase heading not required.)

Army Form C.2118.

2nd Hampshire Rgt   January 1919

Place	Date	Hour	Summary of Events and Information	Remarks and references to Appendices
DHUNN	6th Jan 1919		Usual parade extension, elbow sprints. Football match A Coy. 1 – D Coy. Nil	Nil
DHUNN	7th Jan 1919		Usual parade etc.	Nil
DHUNN	8th Jan 1919		Baths allotted to companies to clean clothing issued – no clothing to clean underclothes issued, new gear 12th. Following officers joined – 2/Lt DORGAN (from H of R) 2/Lt PLANNERY (from H of R) 2/Lt INGLIS 10th (from France)	
DHUNN	9th Jan 1919		2/Lt DORGAN (from H of R) & Brooks arrived on 8th inst. The units of HQ paraded for inspection by the Commanding Officer. Usual parade.	Nil
DHUNN	10th Jan 1919		Usual parade. A lecture was given on Education with Navy' and Army that's well attended	Nil
DHUNN	11th Jan 1919		A Battalion ceremonial parade was held the Colours were on parade, the Bn football team went to WERMELS KIRCHEN to play the 2/7 Hampshire Regt and lost 2 goals to 1. Team were entertained by 2/7 Hants who deserved their win.	Nil

WAR DIARY
or
INTELLIGENCE SUMMARY.

Army Form C. 2118.

3rd Kenneth Rgt

January 1919

(Erase heading not required.)

Place	Date	Hour	Summary of Events and Information	Remarks and references to Appendices
DHUNN	12th Jan 1919		Church parades & in afternoon football match was played YOKELS versus TOWNIES.	nil
DHUNN	13th Jan 1919		The Battalion paraded at 1030 hours and marched to WERMELS KIRCHEN being relieved at DHUNN by 2nd Hampshire Regt. the two Battalions parading each other on the line of march. Billets at WERMELS KIRCHEN are found to be considerably better than those at DHUNN. A Battalion affair was to observe - it is believed for the first time since August 1914 over the duties Mr originated of the N.N.E., NYE M.C. took Battalion from Capt A.H. WHITEHEAD M.C. Usual parades reports.	nil nil nil
WERMELS- KIRCHEN	14th Jan 1919			
"	15th Jan 1919		Usual Parades. Baths allotted to the Battalion, also clean clothing.	nil

WAR DIARY
INTELLIGENCE SUMMARY

Army Form C.2118.

January 1919

Place	Date	Hour	Summary of Events and Information	Remarks and references to Appendices
NERMELS KIRCHEN	16th Jan 1919		All Ranks had the day in billets owing to the severity of the weather.	
"	17th Jan 1919		The Battalion paraded (with Colours) was inspected by Major-General A.E. Confrey C.B.C.M.G. Cdg. 29th Division who presented medal ribbons to Officers & O.R.'s & men photo taken. The following ribbons were presented V.C.'s - 2, B'ar to M.C. - 1, M.C.'s - 6, D.C.M.'s - 2, Bar to D.M.M. - 1, M.M. - 23, French Croix de Guerre - 1, Belgian Croix de Guerre - 2. He afterwards inspected the Transport, workshops, billets etc. of the Battn. expressed himself delighted with everything he had seen. He was particularly pleased with the Transport turnout with the physique, turn out & bearing of all ranks.	
"	18th Jan 1919		Information received that following have been awarded Belgian Croix de Guerre:- Capt. G.E. FARRELL, RSM KNIGHT D.C.M, C.S.M. FENNEL D.C.M, 2/C W. FITZMAURICE M.M. & PTE. M. BYRNE D.C.M. M.M.	

Army Form C.2118.

2nd Leinster Regt

WAR DIARY
INTELLIGENCE SUMMARY.
(Erase heading not required.)

January 1919

Place	Date	Hour	Summary of Events and Information	Remarks and references to Appendices
WERMELS-KIRCHEN	Jan 19		Usual church parade. Baths allotted to Batt. Men delivered shortest sock men received their clothing, and all S.D. Clothing, blankets, greatcoats etc. were delivered. This was necessary.	
"	20th Jan		Usual parade hours.	N/T
"	21st Jan		Several parades. Lecture given by the Adjutant on "The Terms of Re-enlistment" were attended. Lecture on "Australia" given at WERMELSKIRCHEN	N/T
"	22nd Jan		Usual parade hours. Interpreters received visits by word to twice weekly to COLOGNE to talk their dancing officers to the OPERA.	N/T
"	23rd Jan		A cross country run of 2 men per Coy. was held in order to choose a Bn. team. Bn football team went to MULHEIM to play 88th F.A. won 2-0 A lecture on the War through German Eyes given	N/T

2nd Lincoln Regt   January 1915 Army Form 2118.

WAR DIARY
or
INTELLIGENCE SUMMARY.
(Erase heading not required.)

Place	Date	Hour	Summary of Events and Information	Remarks and references to Appendices
WERMELSKIRCHEN	23rd Jan		Usual parades. Lecture to "The German Mentality" given by in the horseman South — 150 men attended, who were delighted with the lecture.	WT
"	25th Jan		Usual parades. Games	WT
"	26th Jan		Divine Service. Hockey match played "Right half" Battalion v. Left half Bn. B Coy recruits beginning the Bn. at association football in Brigade Competition	WT
"	27th Jan		Usual parades. A serious losing competition will supporting & promising material discovered.	WT
"	28th Jan		Usual parades. Games	WT
"	29th Jan		Baths allotted to Bn. No clean clothes. Usual parade	WT
"	30th Jan		Usual parade & sports	WT

2nd Leinster Regt

January 1919 Army Form C2118.

WAR DIARY
or
INTELLIGENCE SUMMARY

(Erase heading not required.)

Instructions regarding War Diaries and Intelligence Summaries are contained in F. S. Regs., Part II. and the Staff Manual respectively. Title pages will be prepared in manuscript.

Place	Date	Hour	Summary of Events and Information	Remarks and references to Appendices
WERMELS-KIRCHEN	31st Jan		Unit parades. Horses & Iris lorries allotted to Bn to send Spectators to BENSBURG to see 86th Bde. Boxing tournament. Cpl. DELANEY 2nd LEINSTER Regt. fought "ROMAN" 2nd RSF (Lytra Heavies) in challenge from Delany - purse £15 = Delaney disqualified in seventh round.	117

N.V. Farrell. Major.
Comg. 2nd Leinster Rgt.

CONFIDENTIAL
===========

WAR DIARY

2nd Battalion The Leinster Regiment.

****

From
1st February 1919
To
28th February, 1919.

****

(VOLUME No. 11)

===

2nd LEINSTER Regt.　February 1919　Army Form C. 2118.

WAR DIARY
INTELLIGENCE SUMMARY.
(Erase heading not required.)

Place	Date	Hour	Summary of Events and Information	Remarks and references to Appendices
NERMELS	1st Feb 1919		Competition in marching, turn-out etc. as preliminary to	
KIRCHEN			Divisional Competition. Route march 5 miles. Points gained by companies as follows:- C Coy -29. D Coy -51. A Coy -76. B Coy -103.	
"	2nd Feb 1919		Usual sports during the afternoon. Divine Service	
"	3rd Feb 1919		The Usual Parades in the morning. Sports in the afternoon were carried out.	
"	4th Feb 1919		Usual parades and sports.	
"	5th Feb 1919		Usual parades etc. Lt Col. H.W. Weldon D.S.O. returned from leave & resumed command 2nd Battalion.	
"	6th Feb 1919		Usual parades. A lecture on "A time Round the Worlds in Wartime" by Major Gilmour attended	

2nd LEINSTER Regt.

February 1919 Army Form C.2118.

WAR DIARY
INTELLIGENCE SUMMARY.
(Erase heading not required.)

Place	Date	Hour	Summary of Events and Information	Remarks and references to Appendices
WERNERS-KIRCHEN	7th Feb. 1919		Usual parades in morning & games in afternoon.	
"	8th Feb. 1919		Commanding Officer's parade in morning. Usual games in afternoon.	
"	9th Feb. 1919		Divine Service. Photo of V.C. D.S.O. Officers at Bde. H.Q. - Gen. Freyberg (with Brig. Gen. B. Freyberg V.C. D.S.O.) Gen. Freyberg left Werners-Kirchen (relinquishing command of the Brigade). The Brigade turned out to give him a final send off. His car was drawn by ropes. Band "2nd" Leinsters played him from the lines. Lt.-Col. Rankin D.S.O. assumed command of the Bgde.	
"	10th Feb. 1919		Usual parades in morning & games in the afternoon. Official photographer took photos of Officers, Sgts., Drums, and each Company.	

2nd Leinster Rgt

Army Form C.2118.

WAR DIARY
or
INTELLIGENCE SUMMARY

(Erase heading not required.)

February 1919

Instructions regarding War Diaries and Intelligence Summaries are contained in F. S. Regs., Part II. and the Staff Manual respectively. Title pages will be prepared in manuscript.

Place	Date	Hour	Summary of Events and Information	Remarks and references to Appendices
WERMERS KIRCHEN	11th Feb 1919		Usual parades and Sports. Yet a draft of 300 volunteers have joined the Battalion.	
WERMERS KIRCHEN	12th Feb 1919		Usual parades & Sports	
"	13th Feb.		Usual parades etc.	
"	14th Feb.		Usual parade etc. Yet there were 178 volunteers on this date & were received in the Battalion. All Officers except Coy Commanders were withdrawn for Service in the Army of Occupation.	
"	15th Feb 1919		Usual parades etc.	
"	16th Feb 1919		Divine Service	

2nd Hants Regt.

Army Form C. 2118.

February 1919

WAR DIARY
or
INTELLIGENCE SUMMARY.
(Erase heading not required.)

Place	Date	Hour	Summary of Events and Information	Remarks and references to Appendices
WERMELS- KIRCHEN	17th Feb. 1919		Usual parades & games. Preliminary bouts for Bde. Boxing Competition. The Battalion won every fight in which it had a representative.	
"	18th Feb.		Usual parades. In the afternoon played 2nd Hampshire Regt. at association football. Draw 1-1.	
"	19th Feb.		Usual parades. Bde. Boxing Competition. The Battalion won three events, viz: Officers. Pte. Donoghue, the Bantams, Cpl. Bowman, the welters, Pte. McAndrews the lights weights.	[signature]
"	20th Feb.		Usual parade. In the afternoon inter-company tug-of-war pulls took place. "D" beat "A" and "B" beat "C".	
"	21st Feb.		Battalion ordered to establish piquets throughout the town DWERMELS KIRCHEN with the object of ensuring that every civilian over 12 years of age is in possession of an identity card. Every house was entered. Some people found without necessary card. "C" Coy relieved the company of the 2nd Hampshire Regt. on outpost duty at THZSPERRE.	

Army Form C.2118.

2nd Lincoln Regt.

February 1919

WAR DIARY
or
INTELLIGENCE SUMMARY.
(Erase heading not required.)

Instructions regarding War Diaries and Intelligence Summaries are contained in F.S. Regs., Part II. and the Staff Manual respectively. Title pages will be prepared in manuscript.

Place	Date	Hour	Summary of Events and Information	Remarks and references to Appendices
HERMELSKIRCHEN	22nd Feb.		C.O's parade in the morning. Hockey match "D" Coy versus "A"+"B" Coys in the afternoon. "D" Coy won 2-1.	
"	23rd Feb.		Divine Service. 2nd Hampshire Regt. were relieved by 2nd/4th Hampshire Regt. The piper of this Bn. played in the 2nd/4th Hants. In the afternoon the Bn. played the 4th Worcestershire Regt. in the 1st round of the Divn. Association Football Competition & after an exciting game won 1-0.	
"	24th Feb.		Usual parades.	
"	25th Feb.		Usual parades. No games owing to wet weather.	
"	26th Feb.		Usual parades. Bn. played 1st K.O.Y.L.I. at Rugby Football at BURG. Lost 13 pts to Nil. The Bn. Concert Party "The Merry Micks" gave a successful performance in the evening.	

WAR DIARY
or
INTELLIGENCE SUMMARY

Army Form C.2118.

2nd Leinster Regt.   February 1919

Place	Date	Hour	Summary of Events and Information	Remarks and references to Appendices
WERMELSKIRCHEN	27th Feb		Usual parades with the morning. In the afternoon the Bn. Association Football team played the 2nd Hampshire Regt. in the 2nd Round of the Divisional Cup and lost 2-1. The Ruffian Concert party gave a performance for our show in the evening.	
"	28th Feb		Bn. engaged on wiring defensive localities in the morning. In the afternoon 6 lorries took spectators to finalists Boxing Competition at the R.G. GLAD BACH	M?

M. Waller Lt Col.
Comdg 2nd Leinster Regt.

28.2.19

2ND LEINSTER REGIMENT.

MARCH 1919
MISSING.

2nd Leinster Regt
2nd Bn THE LEINSTER REGT. 29
April 1919
Army Form 2118

WAR DIARY
or
INTELLIGENCE SUMMARY
(Erase heading not required.)

Place	Date	Hour	Summary of Events and Information	Remarks and references to Appendices
MULHEIM	1st April 1919	—	Usual parades	
"	2nd	—	Usual parades. Warning order received that the Cadre of this Unit will leave MULHEIM on 6th inst.	
"	3rd	—	Usual parades. Notification received of award of the M.M. to Pte. Moffatt V.C.	
"	4th	—	Orders published at Orange	
"	5th	—	Both Allotted to the Battalion. Notification received that all relevant Officers and other ranks not proceeding with cadre are to be sent to No.1 Concentration Camp Cologne for dispersal on 5th inst. Three Officers (Capt. Moran, Lt O'Brien, & Lt. McCullen) and two other ranks proceeded to 5th Royal Irish Regt. Four Officers (Lt. Whittington & Applegard, 2/Lt. Cole, 2/Lt. Dol(?)) and 335 other ranks proceeded to No.1 Concentration Camp for dispersal.	
"	6th	—	The baggage personnel of cadre were en-route to	

2nd Lancs. Rgt.   April 1919   Army Form 2118.

WAR DIARY
or
INTELLIGENCE SUMMARY.
(Erase heading not required.)

Instructions regarding War Diaries and Intelligence Summaries are contained in F. S. Regs., Part II. and the Staff Manual respectively. Title pages will be prepared in manuscript.

Place	Date	Hour	Summary of Events and Information	Remarks and references to Appendices
	6th inst (cont)		COLOGNE Main Station leaving MULHEIM at 0400 hours left COLOGNE at 0245 hours and travelled via DUREN, AACHEN, VERVIERS, and NAMUR to CHARLEROI where the Coy detrained at 2355 hours. Coys entrained	
CHARLEROI	7th inst		Coys entrained at 0100 hours and arrived at its destination WARGNIES-le-PETIT at 0600 hours. The remainder	
WARGNIES-le-PETIT			of the day was devoted to kit-up and cleaning up. The strength of the coy came to 10 officers 401 other ranks.	
WARGNIES-le-PETIT	8th inst		Usual parade etc. The transport and equipment of 2nd Royal Munster Fus was taken over this day.	
"	9th inst		Usual parade James.	
"	10th inst		Usual parades. Played 2-2 R.M.F. at Hockey and won 3-2.	

Army Form C.2118.

2nd Leinster Regt.   April 1919

WAR DIARY
INTELLIGENCE SUMMARY.
(Erase heading not required.)

Instructions regarding War Diaries and Intelligence Summaries are contained in F.S. Regs., Part II. and the Staff Manual respectively. Title pages will be prepared in manuscript.

Place	Date	Hour	Summary of Events and Information	Remarks and references to Appendices
WARGNIES LE PETIT	11th April		Warne parades & games	
"	12th April		Horse parades & games	
"	13th		Divine Service	
"	14th		Usual parades & games	
"	15th		Usual parades etc	
"	16th		Band went to Cambrai framers for 6 days to take part in playing & Massed Bands under Easter Monday.	
"	17th		Usual parades & games	

WAR DIARY or INTELLIGENCE SUMMARY

Army Form 2118.

2nd Leinster Regt.

April 1919

(Erase heading not required.)

Instructions regarding War Diaries and Intelligence Summaries are contained in F. S. Regs., Part II. and the Staff Manual respectively. Title pages will be prepared in manuscript.

Place	Date	Hour	Summary of Events and Information	Remarks and references to Appendices
WARENIES-LE-PETIT	18th April		Usual parades Games.	
"	19th "		Usual parades etc	
"	20th "		Divine Service	XI
"	21st "		Soccer match 1st/2nd Leinster Regt 1st RDF 2nd RDF played in the Semi-final at L'Aunay. During the afternoon Pipe & Drum Bands also played 7th Wills in 1st Round.	
"	22nd "		Usual parades. Played 7th Wills in 1st Round won 4-0.	XI
"			XIII Corps Mortars Competition.	XI
"	23rd "		Usual parades etc.	
"	24th "		Ordinary inspections and parades	XI
"	25th "		Captain Adj. A.E.NYE M.C. proceeded on 14 days leave to U.K. Captain J.H. MONAGHAN M.C. assumes duties of Adj. Battn played 2nd/2nd Northumbrian F.A. in 2nd	XI

WAR DIARY

2ND BN LEINSTER REGT. APRIL 1919

Army Form C.2118.

Place	Date	Hour	Summary of Events and Information	Remarks and references to Appendices
WARGNIES-LE-PETIT	25 April 19		Round Football Competition lost 5-0. Weather unsettled, chilly but no rain.	R
-,,-	26	-,,-	Usual inspection parade. Cadre performed route march of 2 hours duration. Cold day & windy.	R
			Cricket team of 2nd Munsters Fus. and Re Bn. proceeded to LE QUESNOY today to meet 2nd R. Dublin Fus. in friendly hockey match.	
			Result:- Dublin 1 goal Munster Leinster Team 5 goals.	
-,,-	27	-,,-	Divine Service in billets.	R
-,,-	28	-,,-	Usual parades. Rain & snow falling at intervals during the day.	R
-,,-	29	-,,-	Usual parades. Very wet and windy.	R
-,,-	30	-,,-	Inspection parade only. Weather wet and windy.	R

Monaghan. Capt.
Adj. 2nd Leinster Regt.

WAR DIARY

The Cadre of this Btn. leaves COLOGNE Main. Station at 07.00 hrs. tomorrow 6th. inst. and NOT as previously stated. All baggage etc. to be stacked outside Orderly Room by 03.50 hrs. Lorries will leave at 04.00 hrs with baggage and loading party at 05.30 hrs. with the remainder of Cadre.

5.4.19.

[signature]
Captain.
Adjutant, 2nd. LEINSTER REGT.

2. War Diary.

1. The Cadre of this Battalion will leave COLOGNE main station at 0900 hours, tomorrow 6th inst. Destination CHARLEROI.

2. All baggage, officers kits, mess stores etc. will be stacked outside Orderly Room by 0550 hours 6th inst. Four lorries will leave these H.Q. at 0600 hours — three taking baggage and one taking a loading party of 3 N.C.O's & 20 men under the command of Lt. M.C.E. SHARF.

3. Four lorries will leave these H.Q. at 0730 hours taking the remainder of the Cadre personnel.

4. Billets should be left scrupulously clean.

Mulheim
5.4.19

A.D. Hope, Captain
Adjt. 2nd Bn. Leinster Regt.

WAR DIARY

2nd Bn LEINSTER REGT.

Army Form C. 2118.

MAY. 1919.

Sheet I

INTELLIGENCE SUMMARY
(Erase heading not required.)

WO 57

Place	Date	Hour	Summary of Events and Information	Remarks and references to Appendices
WARGNIES LE PETIT	1st May/19	—	Heavy rain during the day. Inspection parade & kit inspection	JR
"	2nd	—	Intermittent showers. Inspection & drill parades during the morning. Three men to UK for 14 days leave.	JR
"	3rd	—	Inspection parade and rifle inspection. Cricket held in the village about noon from 19:30 to 21:30. Opposing team, 2nd Munsters. The cricket proved a success and all ranks had an enjoyable evening.	JR
"	4th	—	Divine Service held in village. Showery during evening.	JR
"	5th	—	Inspection parade. Baths running. Drill. Handling of arms. Dry and bright.	JR
"	6th	—	Inspection parade. Handling of arms and running exercise. Weather continues good. Lieut. & Q.M. Mahony report for leave to UK	JR
"	7th	—	Manual parade. Sports was held at HERBIGNIES today to select competitors for the XIII Corps Athletic Sports to be held on 10th May. The Bn Tug of war team was successful, beating the Signal C.R.E. and 1st Bn Dublin Fus.	JR

2ND BN LEINSTER REGT
MAY 1919. Army Form C. 2118.
Sheet II.

WAR DIARY
INTELLIGENCE SUMMARY.
(Erase heading not required.)

Instructions regarding War Diaries and Intelligence Summaries are contained in F. S. Regs., Part II. and the Staff Manual respectively. Title pages will be prepared in manuscript.

Place	Date	Hour	Summary of Events and Information	Remarks and references to Appendices
WARGNIES LE PETIT.	8th	May 19	Usual parade. Weather condition good. Canine entertainment held in town during evening for the troops.	
-,,-	9th	-	Cadre Coy bathed at LE QUESNOY today.	A/R
-,,-			Usual parade. Cadre played each 7th wilts Regt at cricket today winning by 25 runs.	A/R
-,,-	10th	-	Usual parade. Tug-of-war team and other competitors proceeded to CAUDRY today to take part in XIIIth Corps Athletic Sports.	
-,,-			We won the Tug-of-war after strenuous pull and Bass by Reader obtained 3rd place in the boys race.	A/R
-,,-	11th	-	Divine service held in village.	A/R
-,,-	12th	-	Usual parade. Weather still good. Arms left for demobilization.	A/R
-,,-	13th	-	Usual parade.	A/R
-,,-	14th	-	Usual parade. Capt & Adjt A Nye reported for leave.	A/R
-,,-	15th	-	Usual parade. Games. Weather fine. Three men demobilized.	A/R
-,,-	16th	-	Usual parade - no news. Weather good.	A/R
-,,-	17th	-	Usual parades etc.	A/R

Army Form C. 2118.

WAR DIARY
2nd LEINSTER Regt.
INTELLIGENCE SUMMARY.

MAY 1919.

(Erase heading not required.)

Instructions regarding War Diaries and Intelligence Summaries are contained in F. S. Regs., Part II. and the Staff Manual respectively. Title pages will be prepared in manuscript.

Place	Date	Hour	Summary of Events and Information	Remarks and references to Appendices
Wartois-le-Petit	18th May		Divine Service. The units holidayed in the village for Athletic Sports for evening. Dance took place in the evening. Band of the Regiment attended	An
"	19th May		R. Col. Hon Weldon CBS. Lt Col S. Hollins proceeded on leave to U.K.	An
"	20th May		Usual parades & games. Weather v. good.	An
"	22nd	-	Usual parades & games	An
"	23rd	-	Usual parades etc. Weather excellent	An
"	24th	-	Usual parades etc.	An
"	25th	-	Divine service. Le Quesnoy for R.C's. Band went to Gomegnies to play for R.I.A.	An

WAR DIARY or INTELLIGENCE SUMMARY

Army Form C. 2118.

2nd LEINSTER Regt

(Erase heading not required.)

Place	Date	Hour	Summary of Events and Information	Remarks and references to Appendices
Warfusée le Petit	26th May		Usual parades etc.	An
"	27th May		Usual parade. Corps pic-nic took place in BRMAZ Forest. Ten band boys went from this unit. Enjoyed themselves immensely.	An
"	28th	-	Usual parades etc. Excellent weather.	An
"	29th	-	Usual parades.	An
"	30th	-	Usual parades etc.	An
"	31st	-	Usual parades do.	An

Warfusée-le-Petit
31-5-19

A Murphy Capt / Lt-Col
Commanding 2nd Bn. Leinster Regt

4   2 Times Army Form C. 2118.
                                          29

WAR DIARY
or
INTELLIGENCE SUMMARY.

2nd Leinster Regt.   June 1919   59

Place	Date	Hour	Summary of Events and Information	Remarks and references to Appendices
Winchester Plat	1st June		Divine Service. Capt. J.H. Monaghan left the unit to proceed to U.K.	Closed
"	2nd June		Usual parades etc.	On
"	3rd June		Usual parade. Unit equipment found detailed to remain behind with equipment till sea to U.K. Informed that Capt. will proceed to U.K. without equipment which will follow on without him.	On
"	4th June		Usual parades. Raining.	
"	5th June		Usual parades etc.	On
"	6th June		Usual parades etc.	
"	7th June		Usual parades. V. Warm.	On

WAR DIARY
or
INTELLIGENCE SUMMARY.

Army Form C. 2118.

2nd LEINSTER Regt. June 1919

Place	Date	Hour	Summary of Events and Information	Remarks and references to Appendices
Warpeinel-Pitz	8th June		Divine Service. Warm	On
	9th June		Usual Parade. Received training Weekly	
			Programme.	On
	10th June		Shot runs mail	On
	11th June		Inspection of Regiment by CO	On
	12th June		Usual Parades etc	
	13th June		Draft received. Strength 25 QUEENS for U.K.	On
			on 19th inst.	
	14th June		Usual Parades	On
	15th June		Divine Service	

2nd LEINSTER Regt

WAR DIARY
INTELLIGENCE SUMMARY.

(Erase heading not required.)

Army Form C. 2118.

June 1919

Place	Date	Hour	Summary of Events and Information	Remarks and references to Appendices
Wassigny	16th June		All vehicles & equipment sent to LE QUESNOY.	An
	17th June		Advances withdrawn	
	18th June		All kit etc. packed preparatory to journey	An
LE QUESNOY - CAMBRAI	19th June		Battalion marched from Wassigny-le-Petit to LE QUESNOY where it entrained at 1330 hours to move to CAMBRAI. Strength 4 offrs. 73 other ranks. 6 tons baggage left behind with equipment guard 2 offrs 12 other ranks. Arrived CAMBRAI at 1600 hours and accommodated in Rest Camp.	An
CAMBRAI - BOULOGNE	20th June		Left CAMBRAI at 6700 hours. Arrived at BOULOGNE at 1900 hours. Marched to Rest Camp for the night.	An

2nd LEINSTER Regt. June 1919 Army Form C.2118.

WAR DIARY
or
INTELLIGENCE SUMMARY.

(Erase heading not required.)

Instructions regarding War Diaries and Intelligence Summaries are contained in F. S. Regs., Part II. and the Staff Manual respectively. Title pages will be prepared in manuscript.

Place	Date	Hour	Summary of Events and Information	Remarks and references to Appendices
MULLAGH	21st June		Marched to Demobilization Camp (Marlborough Camp) Boulogne. Arr. Remained there for the day	
	22nd		At Marlborough Camp. Documents clothes clothing etc Ar. Aircrafted & changed etc	
	23rd		Marched from Camp at 0730 to Quay at Boulogne. Embarked for Dover on S.S. Princess An. Victoria. Leaves Boulogne at 0930 hours. Strength 4 offrs. 73 other ranks. 6 tons baggage	

Witmouth
24. 6. 19

A. My Crifton Lt-Col.
Commanding 2nd Bn. Leinster Regt.

www.ingramcontent.com/pod-product-compliance
Lightning Source LLC
Chambersburg PA
CBHW051527190426
43193CB00045BA/2200